When the Apple Falls Far from the Tree

DISCOVERING THE GIFTS WITHIN THE CHAOS

MARGO REILLY

BALBOA.PRESS
A DIVISION OF HAY HOUSE

Balboa Press books may be ordered through booksellers or by contacting:

Balboa Press
A Division of Hay House
1663 Liberty Drive
Bloomington, IN 47403
www.balboapress.com
844-682-1282

Rosemary Sneeringer, Initial Editor
Maria Sultana Mou, Quote Artist

Print information available on the last page.

ISBN: 978-1-9822-7936-3 (sc)
ISBN: 978-1-9822-7935-6 (hc)
ISBN: 978-1-9822-7934-9 (e)

Library of Congress Control Number: 2022901906

Balboa Press rev. date: 02/02/2022

DEDICATION

This book is dedicated to my grandmother, my rock and personal cheerleader for the first twenty-seven years of my life.

To my daughters, so that they may always be reminded they have the strength and courage to persevere.

To myself—never stop believing you are meant for more.

EPIGRAPH

"Because true belonging only happens when we present our authentic, imperfect selves to the world, our sense of belonging can never be greater than our level of self-acceptance."

—Brene Brown

CONTENTS

PART III THE AWAKENING

INTRODUCTION

I AM EVERYDAY PEOPLE. LIKE you, I have a story, one that has been unwritten and waiting to be shared for decades now. I always put off starting things because I am the queen of procrastination. Who knew that a sobriety challenge would give me the clarity and motivation to sit down and finally pour these details onto the page?

I was inspired to begin my writing when I stumbled across a photo on social media that stated, "Trauma is *not* your fault. But healing *is* your responsibility." It stopped me in my tracks. Not only did the words resonate with me; they confirmed that it was time for my book to be birthed. It was time for the healing process to come full circle. I use the term *healing* loosely here, as when the writing all started, I had no idea what I was getting myself into. Unleashing one's childhood trauma is not something to be taken lightly.

I think most would agree that *trauma* is such a broad and loosely used term these days, interpreted differently by many. But I think most would also agree that everyone has some form of it within them, some emotional or physical wound that has kept a part of them from evolving, experiencing, or healing completely.

I've known for most of my life that I would be an author and write a book someday, even though I had absolutely no experience or training as a writer. I knew it would be a memoir with a motivational self-help spin revealing the seasons of my life. There would be reflections of the crazy shit I've experienced, endured, or survived. I also always knew the book could be just as healing for others as it is for me.

My story may not be epic or profound to some; many have been through far worse. Yet, I feel my journey is important enough to be shared and felt. You are not going to find the meaning of life inside these pages. You won't find a definitive solution to your problems, either. I do not hold any type of credentials to be a counselor or a therapist, but I am loaded with life experiences of all sorts. So, what I am hoping you will find here is a connection. If not with the experiences themselves, then by accessing the feelings, emotions, or growth that surrounds them. There is something wondrous about reading words on a page you can deeply relate to, at least on some level. At our very cores, we all seek love, acceptance, and a path made clear. That often happens inadvertently through the connections we make along the way. I feel there is a little something for many of you within these pages.

My life stories are at your disposal. May you take comfort in knowing each and every one of us stems from some level of "fucked-up-ness." It's all about rising above and breaking the cycle versus choosing a lifetime stuck on repeat. In these pages, there are reflections of child abuse, domestic violence, adolescence, emancipation, education, marriage, parenting, cancer survival, alcohol dependency, and a spiritual awakening. Each is a vivid part of my personal story and a progression through my so-called life. They are my truths, the way I remember them to have unfolded. It is not my intention to hurt anyone as I share these raw, personal memories.

It is these truths that have blessed and armed me throughout life with invisible tools that I am forever grateful to have in my arsenal today, many of which I did not know existed until I began reflecting on my life lessons—and many of which you may recognize in your own stories as you read through these pages. This labor of love originally started as a way to export my story from deep within. What I did not know was that an amazing transformation would be born to me in the process.

"I guess I had to go to that place to get to this one." These are words spoken at the start of a song by famous rapper Eminem and that I related to as an adolescent. I have never wallowed in the thought that I was or am a victim; I've known these were life lessons I had to endure for whatever reason. Some were a product of my upbringing, but others were self-inflicted. I did not welcome or come to understand many of them until recent years, when a series of rather unfortunate events would continue to shape and mold the person I am thankful to be today.

Although I felt cheated and disappointed at the lack of a "normal" upbringing and the lack of a caring environment at times throughout my life, I wouldn't trade the outcome for anything. My personal growth and understanding of the ways of the world continue every day, in each moment. In fact, it wasn't until I began writing that I came to understand that each and every season of my life would harvest a silver lining of sorts. A gift.

Halfway through writing my memoir, I stopped and changed the chapters. I needed to outline the hidden gifts we all have the potential to discover if we choose to look at any situation through a new lens. This epiphany came to me like a jolt of lightning as I was driving in the car at Christmastime and the song "The Gift," by Jim Brickman, belted out of my stereo speakers. My ears felt stuck on the ever-repeating verse, "and I'm thankful every day—for the gift." I had been enlightened to the true purpose for birthing this book. And it was suddenly obvious that I would need to share these findings with you, the reader.

By the time I publish this book, I'm sure I'll have another gooey chapter to share. For now, enjoy the snapshots and conversations as I recall my life through my personal lens. Please forgive any colorful language, as it is honestly impossible to tell the story without getting into character.

Welcome to the rediscovery of the "me that I am." This is the transformation and journey I have been called to experience and now share with you.

forgive YOURSELF for not KNOWING WHAT you DIDN'T KNOW BEFORE YOU learned it

— Maya Angelo

PART 1

Growing Up Chaotic

CHAPTER 1

White Trash Reality

I WAS IMMERSED IN A newly released book, a memoir with a self-help spin, much like the one you are embarking on now. The author, Jamie Kern Lima, was giving heartbreaking details of the day she learned she was adopted, a truth she hadn't had the slightest inkling about. Her words were gut-wrenching. Her whole identity was in question. She wondered how this could possibly be happening to her without any prior suspicion.

As the reader on the other side of the page, I struggled to identify. I had spent moments of my life daydreaming about the time someone might deliver that same adoption news to me, providing me with validation of the impossibility of shared bloodlines with the people in my family. Perhaps then, and only then, could I free myself from worrying about turning out just like them.

I cannot tell you the number of times I've heard my colleagues say, "The apple doesn't fall far from the tree." We work in an impoverished small city's school district. It happens to be my hometown, the place where I grew up and still live. Everyone knows everyone, and we are familiar with the families and the struggling students almost from birth. And nine times out of ten, it's a generational cycle we see before us.

Anytime I either hear of or participate in a conversation that includes those words, however, I cannot help but experience some hypocritical guilt. I know firsthand that the apple can and does fall far from the tree every now and then. I am an example. Oftentimes, I interject to say, "Maybe this child will be the one to break the cycle and do amazing things." One can only hope that every child born to adversity will be the exception to the rule. Despite the odds, I have made it my daily task as an educator to remind myself that every child has the opportunity to rise above their means. It has always been my job to help them internalize and believe in that wholeheartedly. Their families do not define them. I teach them that the world can be a loving place, full of opportunity, if we choose to seek out our truest potential. I was not born with this important slice of knowledge. It took learning some terribly hard lessons and a few decades of tucking and rolling throughout life to make sense of it all.

Who am I? Am I who I am meant to be? I buried these deep questions away until recent years. When we pull the thread and unravel ourselves down to the core, who are we really under all those layers? Under all that programming? Under all that we have been exposed to or made to believe?

I am, or at least once was, white trash. Only I clearly did not know this as a child. I do not think I was clued in until I was a young adult. It took some candid later-in-life conversations with a few close cousins to even come to terms with the label. Mind you, it was a label we so willingly placed upon other families, but the truth was, we were the epitome of white trash. Born and raised.

My maternal grandparents and aunts and uncles would sit around the small dining room table in my grandparents' tiny home. They drank beer, chain-smoked cigarettes, spewed obscenities, and preached about how we needed to stay away from this family or that brood. Or they talked smack about the mysterious next-door neighbor who was up to God only knows what. They didn't hesitate to condemn the neighbor lady across the tracks for how many kids she had the nerve to pop out.

I remember listening attentively as a child and taking heed, believing we were above these other families they would gossip about, developing the same opinions as the adults who seemed to know what they were talking about. But the truth is, I now know that *we* were the ones people talked about. *We* were the family with crime, abuse, and skeletons dangling visibly out of the closets. We were the ones people avoided or told their children to stay away from.

Although I didn't come to this conclusion until later in life, my very first dose of this reality came when I was about eleven or twelve years old. There was an ad in the local newspaper seeking a babysitter for hire. I was more than qualified. I was always a natural with young children and played the role of caretaker among my many younger cousins and neighboring kids. With confidence, I dialed the phone number from the ad, thinking I would be able to earn a few extra bucks on the weekend. I chatted with the woman on the other end of the line. She happened to be located a few blocks away, and it made her happy to know I'd be in walking distance. The mother proudly spoke to me about her two children and their likes and dislikes. We planned to pick a day to meet in person.

And then she asked my full name. I said my first and last name aloud over the rotary phone. There was a terribly awkward pause, as if she was covering the phone to speak to someone near her. She got back on the line and distastefully asked, "Um, who are your parents?" I answered the question, and before I knew it, the line was disconnected. She had purposefully hung up the phone and ended our call. I knew this was not a lost connection but rather a lost opportunity because of my infamous family tree. I was embarrassed and mortified, but at the same time, looking back, I completely understand her actions. I probably wouldn't have hired me, either.

This very poignant incident back in my preteen years was my first real lesson in "judging a book by its cover." It is a bittersweet lesson that I will never forget—one that has taught me that everyone should be given a chance, regardless of their roots. And although I am guilty of not always applying this wisdom 100 percent of the time, this knowledge has aided me throughout my adult years, and for that, I am grateful.

Every now and then something will come along to remind me of my white-trash roots. Like the time it showed up while having a conversation with my then seventeen-year-old daughter. She was telling me about something tragic that was happening to a boy in her high school. As she was setting the tone and trying to make me feel the direness of the situation, she said the words, "Mom, you don't understand. He has lived in a homeless shelter. It's bad."

I remember looking up in her eyes and saying, "No. I do understand. You don't know it, but your mother has lived in a homeless shelter before, too." Silence fell over us as she digested this new bit of information. And at that moment, I realized my children knew only a few details of my chaotic childhood. They had absolutely no idea just how horrifically scarred I was and how deeply those traumatic events were rooted.

When we look at the outer surface of a person we know or meet, we innately make a lot of assumptions about their lifestyle, happiness, upbringing, education, and so on. We decide what their life must be like even without having a clue what lies beneath the surface. My own children didn't know what was buried under the surface of their mother's layers. (I kept my background to myself intentionally, as I did not feel they needed to know any of it as young children.)

Around the same time this incident occurred with my daughter, I was texting back and forth with my cousin Heather. (She and I are more like sisters, and our mothers are sisters.) This was when the coronavirus pandemic first struck. She lives down south with her own teenage children. She had posted a picture and a humorous joke on social media about her kids using bread instead of hot dog rolls to eat their hot dogs, as rolls were nowhere to be found in stores. A longtime friend of hers posted a comment underneath the picture, reading something to the effect of, "Oh, Heather, you obviously weren't raised in a trailer park. We ate our hot dogs like that our whole lives."

My cousin now lives quite an affluent life. She has done well for herself in her adulthood. But what this hot-dog commenting southern friend of hers did not know was that my cousin was, in fact, raised in a trailer park for some years as a child. She, too, had grown up pure white trash, though my cousin's friend would not know that by looking at her now. Those roots are buried deep, no longer visible to the human eye. Those roots are also not the type of thing you proudly display or emphasize when building a better life for yourself. She felt compelled to share the screenshot with me as we sporadically share evidence with one another that we were, in fact, white trash for most of our youngest years.

My story will provide a great deal of proof as to how this label was bestowed upon me and my family. You will likely wonder how it could be that I didn't know this information about myself as a child. I guess it is fair to say that I didn't want to believe it. More than anything, all I ever wanted was to have a *normal* family. I knew without a doubt that the things that happened in my home were not happening at my next-door neighbors' houses. However, I have since learned that every family has its own problems. Skeletons are found in everyone's closets. No one is exempt from this truth.

The Gift

> "Forgive those who didn't know how to
> love you. They were teaching you how
> to love yourself." —Ryan Elliott

According to the *Oxford Dictionary* on Google, *self-identity* is "the recognition of one's potential and qualities as an individual, especially in relation to social context." In other words, our self-perceptions.

That makes self-identity a tricky thing, doesn't it? At its root, it is merely a label we slap on ourselves or on those around us. It seems only natural that we would adopt labels that we are familiar with or believe in. But I opted for a better label. I was different. I refused to comfortably identify with the "trash" label I'd been given as a child. Self-perception is one of the most useful tools in our personal human development. It is the leverage you will use to determine who exactly you are and are not.

The beauty of self-identity is that it is fluid. It is full of endless choices and possibilities. We are never stuck "being" one thing or another. As humans, we are given the free will to change our identities as often or few times as we would like. I want to be clear in that, no matter what phase of my life I have passed through, I have never hidden my self-identity. Sure, there were times I wished I was someone else, living someone else's "normal" life. Who hasn't?

I have always accepted and believed that whatever season of life I was living in and identifying with at the time was all part of the plan or the bigger picture. I was born and raised as "white trash." I no longer identify with this lifestyle or way of living. However, I am crystal clear that my life is rooted there, and my tale stems and grows from these poor, unstable beginnings.

the wound IS wound
THE PLACE
WHERE
THE LIGHT
ENTERS
you

—Rumi

CHAPTER 2

Accidentally on Purpose

HAVE YOU EVER THOUGHT THAT it was hard to recall your earliest memory as a small child? It makes sense that it would have to be something either truly amazing or something horribly traumatic to leave a lasting imprint. That's the beautiful and frightening thing about the power of memories. I wish I had a story to insert here that recalls something wonderful and cherished. What I wouldn't give to remember fond memories of my mother or father holding me close with a good book while tucking me into bed. I wish I had even one family photo to reference with the five of us smiling at a photographer. But there is seemingly no evidence that life was ever anything like that in my house. And if there was, I have absolutely no recollection or captured proof of it in my possession.

My earliest memory of life as a child falls in the trauma category. I was *almost* four years old. My very drunk and quite angry father broke my leg. My upper and lower leg bones—to be more specific. Not exactly on purpose. But not exactly on accident, either.

You see, my mother was never home. I mean never. I'd like to say she was gone working long hours to provide for her family.

That, however, would just be another lie. Don't get me wrong; she did work at various restaurants and bars around town—one short-lived late-night job to the next. But most of her time away from being a wife and mother was to fulfill her need of partying and/or cheating.

I remember adoring her when I was very young. She had a simple look that was pretty. She kept herself tidy. Not skin and bones, but not chubby either. She always styled her frosted blonde hair with a curling iron, polished her nails, and had makeup on her face. Cheap perfume lingered from her freshly bathed skin even if it was often masked by the cigarette smoke that followed her like a personal cloud. You could tell she took pride in her looks as she prepared to go out on the prowl. She carried a sense of confidence about her. She knew she could easily get the attention of *someone*. Unfortunately for me, it was not my attention she was seeking. I longed for her time and cuddles more than anything. Let's just say motherhood was not how she was interested in spending her time.

In my younger years, my dad could be described as a gentle giant. He could pass for one of the members of ZZ Top, beard and all. He hung out with some guys in a small local motorcycle gang. Though they sure loved to party back in the day, they were all harmless family guys. He was a hard worker. He labored at a factory just a mile down the road from our house. It was clear that his overnight shifts and overtime hours kept food on our table, paid the bills, and paid for our childcare. When he worked, we had babysitters. Lots of them. A few of them even lived in our home with us for short periods of time.

Our house wasn't big or special, but during those beginning years it felt like a security blanket. A true "starter" home that my grandparents had made the down payment for. It was a tiny two-story dwelling with three small bedrooms upstairs and a master downstairs. I remember the staircase had wooden spindles. I would peek through these as a child when I was supposed to be in my bed fast asleep. My brothers shared a bedroom, and I had one all my own. The extra room was sometimes occupied by a babysitter or a friend of my mother's.

When my mom was at home, you would no doubt catch her cleaning or tidying the place. She was almost OCD when it came to keeping the house clean. You didn't dare walk in the living room with shoes on your feet. Bedding and curtains would be freshly ironed when they came out of the dryer. She painted or wallpapered walls and changed the decor on an almost regular basis even though we didn't really have the money to do so. Everything had its proper place, and despite the fact that we didn't have much money, she would keep the rooms feeling cozy and welcoming. Cleaning and decorating were her forms of therapy. It was her way of escaping her role as a mother to three emotionally neglected children.

On this particular night, my mom was once again gone. My dad was probably at least a twelve-pack deep into his after-work beer ritual. His exhaustion was setting in from his single-parenting gig. Along came a momentary lapse of sanity, and I was unfortunately in the wrong place at the wrong time.

My baby brother and I were in my parents' room, monkeying around on the bed. I was in charge of keeping an eye on him. He was still an infant, just a few months old. My dad was in the living room, which was just on the other side of the wall, either jamming on his guitar or banging the piano, I assumed. Making music was his escape from reality, and he was pretty damn good at it, too. I am sure my sole task on that evening was to entertain the baby and keep him out of my dad's hair. Even at that young age, I recognized the loneliness my dad held in his heart, and I felt sorry for him.

I had heard my irritated father yell, "Stop jumping on that bed!" several times from the other room. I am not sure why exactly I chose not to listen or take heed of the seriousness of his voice. I just continued to bounce my baby brother up and down while he giggled at me with amazement. He loved being with me. Somebody needed me on that day, in that moment.

Out of the corner of my eye, I caught the body language of my now-enraged father stomping toward me at lightspeed. I knew immediately from the scary look he possessed that this was not the gentle drunk my dad usually was when he drank. He lifted me up off that bed. He squeezed and shook me fiercely. Then he tossed me directly up at the ceiling and watched me plummet to the floor below. I hit like a ton of bricks. Every ounce of my little body felt those cracks, and I am more than certain he did, too.

I remember crying out, yelling that my leg was broken and that I couldn't move it. He ignored me. He wouldn't look at me or acknowledge the depth of my pain. I didn't know if he was too drunk or too ashamed of what he had just done—most likely a bit of both. What I do know is I crawled around the house, dragging my limp, lifeless leg, begging for help. That didn't happen until my mother finally arrived home, which of course felt like an eternity.

He must have called her to tell her at least some of the story because when she came through the door, she was already swinging. As soon as she saw me there, she began hitting him and screaming in his face. "What are we going to tell them? What the hell is wrong with you? What did you do to her?"

My mother drove me to the emergency room, which, thankfully was in close proximity to our house. We, of course, quickly rehearsed *the story* on the way there. I was going to tell them about how I did this to myself. It was an accident. The broken bones and immense pain were my own fault, brought about from my unfortunate tumble off the bed that I was recklessly bouncing on. And upon arrival, it went just like that. They took the story for gold and did not give it a second thought. *Really?* I could see a possible broken bone from falling off a bed. But I had two broken bones being repaired. *No one was suspicious? Was I that convincing?*

That damn cast was molded to go from the tip of my toes all the way up to the top of my hip. It was heavy as hell, not at all like they make them today. It probably weighed more than I did. I remember it vividly because it was summer. My skin sweated profusely during those weeks. I loathed that cast. It was a constant reminder of that horrible night when my father snapped into someone I had never seen before. It stole away my ability to have summertime fun like all the other kids. I had to take sponge baths because I couldn't be submerged in water. When they finally cut the damn thing off weeks later, a collection of objects fell out from inside. Out poured pencils, barrettes, and straws that I had used to try to itch my discomforts away.

Sadly, the sting of that awful day in my parents' bedroom lingered on. Just a few weeks later, it would be my fourth birthday. My July party took place in our backyard. It was a typical hot summer celebration, complete with a kiddie pool and water fun. Back in those days, summer birthday parties weren't just for the kiddos. Tons of adults were invited to join the celebration as well. Pretty sure my entire neighborhood was there that day. I watched cautiously from the sidelines with my full-leg cast and crutches as all the sun-kissed kids and cousins splashed and played in the water to stay cool. The adults casually passed around their rolled marijuana joints while feasting on picnic food throughout the day. If they weren't smoking pot, then there was always a cigarette hanging out of their lips or being clamped between their fingers. Everyone smoked back then, including both sets of my grandparents. Adults fussed to make sure the ice was constantly replenished to keep the keg of beer ice cold. It was my mother's mission on my birthday to keep the plastic cups filled and the entertainment flowing. Everyone was content. Everyone, that is, except for me.

That is my earliest memory of this lifetime. Traumatic, yes. You should know, however, that my father never hurt me physically again. It wasn't in his nature to lash out as he did that evening. And the damage was clearly enough to keep him from ever doing such a thing again. I wish I could say it was also enough to stop the uncontrollable drinking, but then how would he deal with his missing-in-action wife? The drinking most certainly continued, always until he passed out, and whether or not he had to work the next day. This was daily life in our house.

I don't recall a single cherished or fond memory of my life when my parents were still together. I don't ever remember being a family or doing things as a unit. When I was a young child, there was ever only one adult in the house tending to us at a time. (Thank God for that.) Either he took care of us, the babysitters were there, or—on rare occasions—my mom was home while he was off to work.

I do recall finding a photograph once before when I was very young. It appeared that we were at a local amusement park. But that picture is long lost, like all other evidence of us as a family.

The Gift

> "The wound is the place where the
> light enters you." —Rumi

There are so many things in life that can be both a blessing and a curse. Detachment is one of them. I believe it was this early time in my life when I began to master the skill of removing myself from the situation. Cutting the cord so to speak, from those who were unable to love and care for me in the way I deserved and needed.

My imagination was my best friend as a young child. And I was not afraid to use its easily accessible scenery as a safe haven or to escape from my reality. Instead of pondering the questions *Why is this happening to me?* and *What am I going to do?* I spent time dreaming in a place where these questions and answers were unimportant and never even considered.

My detachment from unthinkable situations and people had actually sparked the growth of my inner world, as I had an innate sense of knowing that life didn't have to be this way. My life would not be this way. Even though I was not practicing religion, there was never a time in my life when I didn't feel as if some larger force was ultimately in charge of my care and well-being. I had a sense of protection that shielded me even if it wasn't coming from the caretakers in my life.

Detachment ultimately became the premise for my belief and understanding in faith and in a higher power. I would also discover in my later years that it would be the very tool needed to get me through some unexpected, unendurable hardships.

I guess the difficult part is learning the genius behind it, when to use it constructively, and when it needs to be noticed and halted in its tracks.

when

SOMETHING

FEELS *off,*

it **IS**

—Abraham Hicks

CHAPTER 3

The Devil Himself

SADLY, AS HARD AS I may try to recall any moments of happiness in my childhood home, I am unable to do so. It is impossible to overlook the scarring events that took place inside those walls. Miserable moments simply outweighed any sincere or lasting flashes of nurturing, if there even were any. My mother was not warm or tender. I spent many of my youngest years crying at the doorway, whimpering like a little puppy as she would leave. Who could possibly know my troubled early years with my mom and dad would be welcomed in comparison to what lurked just around the corner? The real nightmare began when I was about six years old and in the first grade.

I first met Gary on a side street near my home. I was riding my bicycle around the block by myself, which was typical for a sunny day in my neighborhood back then. A car crept down the brick road beside me, following along slowly as I peddled. It was like watching an abduction go down on the big screen.

The car was long and bronze in color, much like the thousands of freckles splattered all over his face and body. He hung halfway out of the vehicle, arm dangling loosely on the door. *Was he planning to use this hand to pull me off my bicycle?* His teeth were extremely crooked, and he gave off an uncomfortable vibe. His head was mostly bald and rather sunburned. Actually, all of his skin was tinted red. The fumes from the car exhaust polluted the air around us. I felt instantly petrified and uncomfortable in his presence and his sleazy stare. Hair rose on my sweaty neck, and I had to remind myself to breathe.

And then my name rolled casually out of his mouth. "Are you Margo? Is your name Margo?" he asked.

I stopped my bike and stared back, focusing on the eyes of this strange man who felt comfortable enough to approach me. I think I nodded even though I had no intention of engaging in any sort of conversation with such a creep. He told me his name was Gary and that he was friends with my mommy. Then he proceeded to watch me in his rearview mirror as the car inched forward ever so slowly. He had clearly stopped to check me out and make his presence known. I felt tremendous relief when the car disappeared down the street, and I looked down to see my hands clenched tightly around my handlebars and my feet frozen to the cement. Thank God he wasn't a predator. *Or was he?*

I cannot remember if I ever asked my mom about this encounter when I got back to the house. She probably wasn't home, anyway. But I did see that son of a bitch again soon. Who knew it would be in my own bedroom? Thank you, Jesus, he was not there to prey on me. My rather naive mother, however, had surely fallen victim.

I was deeply asleep in my bed, and I'm guessing it had to be two- or three o'clock in the morning. My mother, of course, was just getting home from God only knows where. Reeking of booze, she tapped me awake. She told me to get out of my bed and go sleep with my brothers in their room. I was confused as I squinted up at her, but I was also too tired for any of her shenanigans. I got up and did what I was told. I dragged my half-asleep body down the hallway toward my brothers' doorway, and that is when I saw him again. Gary, the creep. Turns out, my mother was sneaking him into our house for a little rendezvous like a wild teenager.

Was my father home? Why, of course he was, fast asleep in the room exactly below mine. I am sure she counted on his daily beer-drinking to keep him snuggled in bed and out cold while she did the deed. He had no clue about the sins taking place just a few feet above his head. I, on the other hand, knew exactly what was happening in my bed at the ripe age of six. We were all exposed to quite a bit at an early age. My mother, as I've mentioned, did not shelter us from anything. She'd openly walk around stark naked in front of us. We knew what her body parts were and what they were used for. Most of that was because of our frequent exposure to R-rated television. We were never asked to look away or get lost when inappropriate flicks flashed on the TV screen. I knew what "love-making" scenes looked and sounded like, just like I knew what a bludgeoned horror scene looked like.

I could validate the sounds coming from my own bedroom that evening without a shadow of a doubt. I knew entirely way too much for a child my age. I had already seen "oops sex" up close and personal and also by curiosity. I was about five years old when I peeked through a keyhole during one of my mom's parties. One of our babysitters was using my mom's bed to get it on with a party goer. I knew I shouldn't be peeking, but my curious little mind couldn't miss an opportunity to see firsthand what all the noise and fuss was about. It sounded like this stranger was hurting her, but clearly, he was not.

As I drowned out the sinful sounds that late evening, I knew one thing was for certain: our family would never be the same again. If she had the nerve to sneak this scumbag into our home, things could only go downhill from here. And they did.

The next thing I knew, my father's entire life was being thrown onto our front lawn in broad daylight. Everything from clothes, to instruments, to personal belongings. It was all there on display for the whole neighborhood to see. Imagine his surprise when he pulled in from work that day, as if he had done something to deserve being chased out of his own home—the one who worked his tail off to provide for us all those years. This is when I knew for the very first time that my mother was mentally ill and extremely selfish. She was always only out for herself and simply did not care who she hurt in the process or if she lost people along the way. It was the first time I felt real resentment toward her, even though I had been let down many times before. I am the daughter of a narcissist, one of many titles she'd come to earn from me and everyone who knew her. The coming years would easily affirm the ill feelings I had brewing toward my mother and her poor choices in life.

I often wondered why she was the way she was. She had such a close relationship with both of her parents. She and my grandmother did things together often. They booked their hair appointments together. They cooked together. They went to BINGO together. When my mom was done cleaning and ironing at our house, she would go and do the same at her parents' home. My mom felt an obligation to take care of them, and that feeling was visibly mutual among them. Her parents would come to her rescue many, many times from this point forward.

The beatings began almost instantly. My mother had opened the door and allowed the devil himself to nestle inside our quaint little home. I would later learn that she knew damn well what she was getting herself into, as she was warned of his past. He was a woman beater and a home wrecker with years of proof. Yet my mother was willing to gamble and take the chance that she might be the one to change his sadistic ways.

I'd watched a drama on TV once where a therapist was counselling a battered wife. As she chipped away at the woman's hardened outer shell, they both came to the realization that she was just as sick as her husband. Wanting to be brutalized and punished was just as ill-natured as the need to inflict pain upon another human being.

You may be thinking that nobody asks to be beaten and brutalized. But that would just confirm how little you may know about the realities of domestic violence. Of course, there are cases when it is totally one-sided. But in many cases, you will find it is an absolutely orchestrated, toxic dance between two severely mentally ill people. This was most certainly the case and the repetitive scene that was about to play out for the next decade or so of my mother's life.

We would beg for mercy, crying out loud for her to stop provoking the situation. She seemed to get off on poking the bear. We urged her to walk away and let it be. But she was quite literally incapable. She would talk back with a vicious tongue, begging for more. She would lash out verbally for what felt like an eternity to keep the angst alive and thriving. Bloodshed was inevitable. In fact, these situations usually did not stop unless they required medical attention or were broken up by local police. They were at our house on a daily or a weekly basis. Surely the neighbors were just as tired of hearing it as we were. Our dishes and furniture all bore the evidence of battle wounds. So much for the pride and labor she had once put into her pretty papered walls. They now had gaping holes pierced through to the other side, visual reminders of their fearless feuds—much like the scars they would leave on our little hearts. There were many episodes where stitches would be necessary, and her mouth was even wired shut once because of how badly he broke her jaw.

This was the new life that my mother willingly discarded our father for. She moved Gary in just moments after sprinkling my father's belongings out onto the lawn. She didn't have a single care in the world that her three children were now going to be living an actual nightmare. I was about seven years old at this time. My older brother was nine, and my little brother was just about four.

I later learned that my mom met this monster at the bar where she worked, called Time Warp. Who knows how long the affair had been going on before he moved in? It's not like there weren't others before him. My mom was well-known for being promiscuous. Luckily, I hadn't met or encountered any of her other lovers. And I wish to hell I had never been introduced to this one. He would prove to be the sickest son of a bitch I have come across to date. I am happy to report that he never physically accosted me, but he absolutely annihilated my family, my home, and my idea and sense of "normalcy." He took away the comfort and protection I had once felt within my house, even with dysfunctional parents. He stole the thoughts and contentment in my head. And for what it's worth, he stole the tiny remaining parts of my mother's love. She had nothing left to give after her entanglement with him. He siphoned every bit of her away and her life force energy would never come back—not that I have much to refer to prior to his arrival.

The Gift

"When something feels off, it is."
—Abraham Hicks

Do you trust your gut? Does your intuition show up in a moment's notice to tell you what you need to know? I lost touch with my intuition and inner knowing for much of my adult life. (More on that in a later chapter.) But as a child, my innate sense of knowing and trust was at its strongest. I am willing to bet that is the case for most of us. I often had premonitions and would then be mind-blown when I saw them come to light, especially if I had shared the prediction out loud with someone.

I relied heavily on first impressions and have always had the ability to read people like a book. As a child, when I looked at a person, I felt as if I could see past their eyes and into their soul. I, of course, did not know this way back then. But even still today, when I look into a person's eyes, it feels deep, regardless of who they are and how long I've known them. (And I will admit that, throughout the years, this has gotten me into trouble by sending some false signals as well.)

As this deep, intuitive skill was building in me as a child, I learned to trust no one until they made a case for themselves. And I don't consider this a bad trait, but rather a useful tool to have acquired. It wasn't that I mistrusted everyone around me. I frankly had an internal scanning system that could weed out the kind and generous from the total assholes I would encounter throughout my life. They say the gut never lies, and I had plenty of concrete evidence in my first decade of life to prove this theory to be absolutely true.

Just because EVERYTHING's DIFFERENT doesn't MEAN ANYTHING HAS CHANGED

—Irene Peter

CHAPTER 4

Kidnapped and Robbed

AS IF LIFE ON DOWNING Lane was not screwed up enough, our existence was about to turn up a notch.

You wouldn't suspect a thing. The way we walked with chips on our shoulders sprung invisible shields around us. A protectant of sorts.

It was a quaint little neighborhood in Florida, just outside of the Orlando area. Circled rows of ranch-style houses surrounded a manmade lake. Our new address was visible just ahead. It was a Spanish-style home. The exterior was slathered in cream-colored concrete, fitting, since there was no doubt that we were prisoners once we were inside the doors. It was hot and sticky outside, something my northern skin was not happily adjusting to. My brothers and I were coming home from our new elementary school just a few blocks away, passing unfamiliar territory, unfamiliar neighborly faces, and unfamiliar sights and sounds.

We approached our house—a rental, of course, sparsely furnished and lacking anything inside that made it feel even a little bit like home. It was not only mostly empty but eerily quiet on this day as we passed through the arched concrete doorway and into the abyss of our fresh new hell. We could hear faint sobbing coming from the master bathroom. The tears belonged to my mother. This was pretty much a daily ritual for her, but today something felt and sounded different. Her sobs were deep and haunting, and I knew it meant she was dealing with more than the typical slapping around or whacks upside the head. Why did she continue to subject herself to this way of living? More importantly, why were we being forced to live an unhappy life alongside her?

Instinctively, we banged on the door, trying to get inside. My mother's newly acquired husband, Gary, was not around at the moment. To this day, I cannot understand why on earth she would officially tie the knot. But if memory serves me well, it was for insurance purposes. She murmured words for us to *go away* or something to that effect. But the doors were cheaply made, and my older brother knew just how to stick a pointy object through to release the lock on the other side. The door easily flew open to unveil an awful scene that I wish I could erase from my mind: My mother had slit her wrists with a razor. The metallic smell of blood hung in the humid air. It ran down her wrists and fingers as she sat on the closed toilet, hunched over the bathroom sink. There was so much blood, I was sure we'd witness her last breath right before our very eyes.

A normal child may have panicked. A typical child might have raced to the phone to dial a 911 emergency, but I did not. I stood there frozen. My immediate thoughts at the ripe age of nine years old were, *You selfish-fucking bitch!* How could this so-called mother of mine be trying to kill herself, only to leave us here in this mess she created, deserting us to be with the lunatic monster she had chosen to fall in love with and marry? *Are you fucking kidding me?*

Don't get me wrong. As a child, I had great big heart. I am still a raw, emotional person. But part of me secretly wished on that day that it all could have ended right then and there, that my brothers and I could easily be turned over to Child

Protective Services and shipped back to New York, the place where we belonged, with a life and an extended family waiting for us.

But it didn't go that way at all. Turns out, it was a plea for attention. My mother cleaned up the superficial wounds she dug into her wrists that day, not deep enough to welcome her death or even to warrant stitches. Rags would do the job to halt the bleeding until she could tape herself up with makeshift bandages. And chaotic life as we knew it just continued as if the moment had never even happened to her. Or to us.

We picked squeamishly at our dinner later that evening without a single reference to the episode just hours beforehand. We were all so good at pretending and faking it. We didn't dare ask questions. Who were we to share our feelings or opinions? It's not as if we mattered. Never mind the fact that we had literally been kidnapped, uprooted from our home and family in New York without a single hint or warning. Now that I think of it, we never knew what the day would bring upon arrival at home. School had become a true sanctuary for me, a place of peace in my early childhood. A place I longed to be. You can imagine the dread that came upon us as we left school and got closer to the doors of our home each day knowing what was likely to happen.

Moving to Florida happened out of nowhere. I vividly remember the day we arrived home from school, midafternoon. In front of our house was a U-Haul truck that was preloaded with all of our belongings. One minute I was skipping joyously home to play, and the next, I was literally being placed into the moving truck like a box myself. Creepy Gary hit the gas, and the truck lurched forward. I had not a single clue where we were going or why, for that matter. It felt like it all happened in a matter of seconds.

While we headed South down the interstate, she spoon-fed us with clues of excitement. Then she proclaimed, "We're moving to Florida!" like we were winning the Disney lottery or something.

My thoughts raced with both fear and excitement. *A happy new beginning? Things will be different? A place just down the road from Mickey Mouse himself? Could this really be true? Sounds dynamite!* Or at least it probably did for the first hour or so of that dreaded two-day trek down the East Coast.

Turns out, her new love had found some construction work down where his brother was already living. You could see my mother truly hoped in her bones that this was going to be a great new beginning. An escape away from their current toxic environment, away from the strain of their exes and all who knew their violent, wicked ways. A fresh new start. Surely relocating would make everything better. How lovely of them to bring us along for the ride. I am convinced the motivation behind dragging us along was solely her financial dependence on our support check from my father each week.

As I mentioned, the move came out of nowhere, smack dab in the middle of a school year. I was in the fourth grade and we didn't get to say goodbye to anyone. Our move was clearly kept a secret for a reason, as we would later learn my poor father hadn't had a clue. He tried tirelessly to locate our whereabouts. However, in the mid-'80s, the internet and GPS were still aspiring thoughts, at least to the mainstreamed world. His only leads were the lies my mother told her family and close friends. Since my dad didn't have thousands of dollars to pay a private investigator, he really didn't have any options. To this day, I cannot believe the police or Child Protective Services didn't step in and help to locate us for our safety. Then again, they didn't save us from all the gore and bloodshed we had already faced, so why would they now? We became the white trash family in another state. We had no idea whatsoever what misery lay ahead.

After the two-day journey that physically felt like ten, we finally arrived in the Sunshine State. Upon pulling up, we received news that our new home was not ready just yet. So, all our furniture and bulky belongings were placed in a storage unit for the time being. Clothing, our most beloved toys, family photo albums, and documents remained in boxes with us. Our family of five crammed into my step-uncle's mangy little apartment. I guessed a few days of waiting wouldn't be the end of the world. It was dirty and gross and almost intolerable. I did, however, make a mental note that the neighborhood itself wasn't so bad and felt safe-ish.

Although I had visited Florida a time or two in my younger years, this was my first encounter sharing a living space with cockroaches—an infestation of them. We northerners are not used to living among so many insects. I cried my little self to sleep every single night, afraid to open my mouth for even a breath of air. It was torturous. My mother kept assuring us this was just temporary and that we would soon fall in love with the new place when it was ready. But all I could think about was how, just days before, I was nestled in my own bedroom back in New York. My instincts firmly warned me that this wouldn't be the worst of it. Even though my mother had arrived with high hopes, I could tell she was being plagued with doubts as well. She wore worry on her face instead of lipstick during these years.

About a week or so later, we found ourselves sleeping elsewhere—only not by choice. My loving stepfather, Gary, had christened our new life in Florida with the typical, brutal beating my mother got on the regular, right there in his brother's apartment. Even with his brother screaming at him to stop. Only there was no stopping him once the first punch was thrown. Objects were flying and smashing all around. As usual, the three of us kids had front row seats for the show. Thank goodness some close neighbors were getting an earful and called it in immediately. Of course, they weren't aware of our history. Neither were the local police. We were loaded safely into the back of a patrol car, delivering us kids and our mother to a shelter for homeless and battered women.

Looking back, I am grateful for their care and intervention.

The police back home in New York never attempted to rescue us or even relocate us. Domestic disputes had some pretty lax rules back then. In New York, she was the mother and the homeowner, and that bought her entitlement to us. But here in the Sunshine State, we were just guests without any real address to claim as ours.

I don't recall much about the shelter other than the shame and embarrassment I felt for being there. I'm sure it was written across my face. *How could this be happening? How could this continue? Wasn't this supposed to be our new happily ever after in the land of the Magic Kingdom?* The pain in our eyes was never, ever enough for her. Like a skipping vinyl record, the vicious cycle was stuck on repeat. We would watch her get brutalized and cry out loud for it to stop. She would stare right through our cries for mercy as if we weren't even there as witnesses. On most occasions, it would take only hours for her to forgive him and move on like nothing had ever happened. Makeup and bandages would barely do their job of covering her wounds before fresh ones would arrive in a new location just a day or two later. *How did we get here? How did this become our life?*

Being exposed to this horror flick made me grow up entirely too fast. I couldn't help but tune in with attentive ears and observing eyes. I recorded all the little details deep down inside each scar that adorned me emotionally. This wasn't love. This wasn't parenting. This most certainly wasn't happily ever after. This wasn't the way my life was supposed to be. *Or was it?*

Turns out, staying in the shelter for a few days would not be the most upsetting memory of that particular episode. Returning to the mangy apartment where we were staying at the time was. We stayed in the shelter while they tended to my mother's wounds and healing. When it was time for us to be released, a volunteer from the facility loaded us into her car. She had the wonderful task of returning us to the apartment where Gary may or may not be found. The volunteer engaged in small talk with my mother about next steps to keep "safe" and where she should call if we found ourselves in despair again. *We could surely count on that.* She pulled in front of the rental house to let us out, but we were completely distracted by what was going on just a couple driveways down. It was a corner store of sorts, with a big dumpster out back that was exposed to the street corner we were parked on. There were a handful of people swarming around it. Some were rummaging through the contents while others were walking away with items. It took all but a split second for us to realize they were looking through our personal belongings.

Our toys, our clothes, our keepsakes—you name it. That sick bastard had tossed every single item we had into the giant garbage dumpster. What's even worse was that we were too late. Ninety-nine percent of it was already gone. My mother began yelling for the people to stop, physically pulling our last few possessions from their hands. We cried helplessly from the sidelines, covering our eyes in deep, deep shame and sorrow, but nothing was left. Even family photo albums of our school pictures had been taken. They were gone. Just like my childhood.

Why did any of us believe for even a second that this move would make anything different? He was still the exact same man, no matter what the coordinates on the map read. Just weeks before they had dragged us down to Florida for this "new life" experiment, we had encountered what I thought would be the worst of him—an incident that should have had his ass locked behind bars for a good amount of time. It was a scene that should have made my mother call it quits for good, and one where we should have been permanently removed from that volatile home—the home where we were subjected daily to violence and corruption that no child should ever see.

We were in the upstairs bedroom in our New York home, the room that belonged to my brothers. My youngest brother and I were huddled close to my mother. Directly across from us, leaning against the wall, was the lunatic, Gary, who held a shot gun pointed in our direction. As small children, we were obviously petrified that this asshole might accidentally shoot and kill one of us. My mother, thankfully, had phoned the police for help when she knew his level of rage was taking on new heights. Several cop cars were parked out front, and officers were walking circles around our house. She had told them that he had a gun on us, as they immediately treated this as a hostage situation. Hostages we were, indeed. We were hostages to the tainted, sickened love these two sociopaths felt for one another.

I remember the police repeatedly yelling through a megaphone to make verbal contact with them while trying to diffuse the situation. With his typical shit-eating grin, Gary pointed the gun at us and threatened that we had all better keep our mouths shut. I could not help but wonder if we'd be the next family featured on a special episode of the show *20/20*: "Man Shoots and Kills a Mother and Her Small Children." He watched carefully out the window with one eye to gauge their proximity. It was clear that a plan was brewing in his crazy mind. The next thing I knew, he slowly lifted the window and perched his body on the sill. Leaving the gun on the floor in front of us, he leaped through the air and onto our neighbor's roof. Luckily for him, the house was only about six feet away from ours. He then tumbled over the roof like Spider-Man himself, disappearing into thin air. Not one cop claimed to have seen it happen. And just like that, he was gone. Escaped. *Poof*—like magic.

By then, he knew the routine: stay away a day or so while my mother withdrew from the drug that he was. When he returned, she would undoubtedly forgive him, acting like nothing ever happened so she could get her fix again. No charges would be filed because she had the power to say no to domestic charges in those days. If she ever did have the balls to have him arrested, she always dropped the charges the following day. He knew he could count on this.

Who in the hell was in charge of protecting us, anyway? This man, as damaging, disgusting, and violent as he may be, was her everything. She held him on a pedestal. Our lives revolved around him in every possible way. I was a mere nine or ten years old when they uprooted us and snuck us away to Florida in the U-Haul that day. Though we were just young kids, we knew we were there for the money. The two of them could never financially make it work without the help of my father's support checks that they counted on each week. We even overheard them argue about that a time or two.

Thankfully, life in Florida was short-lived. Police visits had quickly become the norm, even in a fresh new state. Their screaming matches alone were enough to warrant someone dialing the cops. The neighbors were not nearly as willing to put up with the lovebirds' predictable bullshit. It was six months or so before we hightailed it back to New York. My mom had no access to family and friends to come to her rescue that far away, and she soon realized she wouldn't be able to make the Sunshine State work after all.

But our trek back to New York didn't happen until one last made-for-TV incident occurred at a local corner convenience store. I believe it was a 7/11. It was late and quite dark outside. The two of them were aggressively arguing in the parked car with us three children in tow in the back seat. A Florida police car soon showed up, and then another and another. Six officers had made a semicircle around Gary after asking him to step out of the vehicle. They began probing him with questions, and I could see his face flush with blood and his veins begin to bulge. The glow of the parking lot lights shone on him like a stage spotlight, and his rage began to surface. I was distinctly familiar with what came next, and this night would be no exception.

An altercation began. Six grown men in uniform tried to pin Gary down in his rage and fury. He swung and fought and took some good hits. And then, he successfully managed to free himself from their grip and run away. I watched the officers disperse in all sorts of directions, anticipating his next move. But that sly son of a bitch escaped yet again, disappearing into thin air like Houdini. He was nowhere to be found, even with serious manpower on this hunt. It was unbelievable to witness, but then again, why would I be surprised? I'd seen this disappearing act before, just months earlier.

I learned as they reconvened and spoke out loud with my mother that he had several warrants stemming from the state of New York. (No wonder we had left so quickly the day we moved!) When the store clerk called in the car's license plate, the police were quickly informed about who they were coming to deal with. Hence, three cop cars and six officers.

I remember having feelings of disappointment and defeat pour over me that evening. It weighed on my heart like a ton of bricks. I wanted them to catch Gary so badly, to take him away from us for as long as possible—hopefully forever. I wanted my family and my life back. But after seeing him fight off and escape all these strong officers, I knew my mother was doomed. I knew we were doomed. Any hope I had clung to up to that point left altogether that evening.

Turns out, we ran out of lifelines in Florida. A day or two later, Gary magically resurfaced. We were instructed to wake up and pack up our belongings quickly. An immediate feeling of relief took over my body. Was it too good to be true? I missed the old, familiar chaos of life in New York. At least family, friends, and neighbors were there when their situations would ensue. I considered us lucky to move back into our small, two-story home in our familiar little neighborhood on Downing Lane. Thankfully, my mother had enough sense to rent our home out only on a short-term basis. I'm guessing that deep down, she knew a new life was not waiting for her down south—or anywhere else, for that matter. The house on Downing Lane was the only constant in her life and would be for decades to come.

The Gift

"Just because everything is different doesn't
mean anything has changed." —Irene Peter

You might think it hard to find any sort of gift in all the
mayhem and misery that the first decade of my life presented. But
I was actually being prepped for one of life's most essential survival
skills: resilience. Resilience is a coping skill or mechanism that
encompasses many others, such as tolerance, endurance, pliability,
adaptivity, strength, and hardiness. These were all things I had
practically mastered by the age of ten.

Although I would have traded that life in for something better
in a heartbeat at the time, I have profound gratitude now for the
foundation that my miserable childhood had laid. Is this an ideal
way to learn resilience? Of course not. I am sure there are much
better paths to becoming resilient, but I am also willing to bet
that not one of those paths comes with ease and comfort. It's not
a secret that life's mishaps and soul-crushing events are those that
plant the seeds for the development of this essential life skill.

It's fair to say my resilience grew like a wild weed in a sunny
pasture. It was fertilized on almost a daily basis, and I began to
make tough decisions about what I was or wasn't going to allow
in my life from that point forward. I learned that the only person
I could ever depend on was myself—a belief that still rules my
thoughts and actions today.

I am not WHAT happened to ME. I AM WHAT I choose To BECOME

—Carl Jung

CHAPTER 5

Subjected

IF YOU AND I WERE nestled in the corner of a restaurant and we were asked to observe all that we could for five minutes, using our senses and then write about it, we would be astounded at the different outcomes written on that paper. Perhaps I would be more focused on the visuals, whereas you may be keener about the smells and sounds. This, my friend, is perception. It's another one of those things I would come to understand more clearly as time marched on.

Perception is not just how we see things with our eyes. In fact, the *Oxford Dictionary* describes it as: "The process of becoming aware through the senses. Or Intuitive understanding and insight."

When I apply this knowledge now, I am fully able to understand that what I am writing about is my own personal take on things, the way things unfolded through my senses. Let's throw in the fact that I am a natural-born empath. As an empathetic person, I have all the feels and raw emotions. Not only do I have those that belong to me; I also feel those of every single person I come into contact with. That means I felt every blow to my mother's face. I deeply felt the rejection I would see in her eyes every time I would beg for her to stop taunting him and she would refuse my request by looking away.

What continued to happen in the next several years of my childhood is nothing short of a *Jerry Springer* episode. You cannot make this stuff up. The scenes and scenarios are so ridiculous and far-fetched at times that they seemed to be make-believe even to me, like I was living somebody else's life. I wish I could say that was the case, but these are my embedded mind movies. Little flashbacks to a childhood of horror, sadness, and neglect.

I started to see and pay for a certified counselor the exact same week I began writing this book. I knew for certain it was going to be a tough task facing the demons of my past. I knew for certain I would be unleashing my sweet inner child, who longed so painfully for a mother and father who would love and notice her. I also knew certain things would come up that I had long forgotten and suppressed, yet it was still a task I was ready for. Healing through my writing has always been in my cards. My inner self confirmed that the time was now. My motivation in booking that appointment was to seek guidance for all the feelings that were about to flood to the surface.

As I began recalling incidents that I had faced as a child, I wanted to convince myself that I was making things up or that maybe I was remembering it all wrong. It would certainly be easier to accept that these things were fictional or overly exaggerated. But I assure you—even though it is told through my own personal storytelling—these are astounding truths I dare to share. These things did, in fact, happen. I bet there are even more instances that I will recall as time goes on. These memories are simply the most profound ones that have come to light to be healed.

To complete strangers, I imagine we looked like a semi normal family of five. But to the locals, we were one of the very first families to have an actual nasty divorce take place and a stepparent enter the picture. Judgement and disdain came from all directions as we became the poster people for what a "broken home" looked like. There were stepchildren involved on both sides for my parents, although I don't remember Gary's kids ever being around. I am guessing his ex-wife successfully kept him out of the picture via court orders. As children, we knew one thing was certain: what we thought or felt did not matter. We did not have much choice but to accept the fact that this was part of our life now. The same went for my dad, who had moved just miles down the road when my mom discarded him a couple of years earlier. He soon found a new love interest as well. It was established through the court system that we would have weekly visitations with him and his newly acquired family on Saturdays. Sometimes we were allowed to go; other times, my mother would use us as leverage against him and not allow it, just to be spiteful. My dad would phone the police, as she was violating a court order, but it was never enforced. They would knock on the door as my dad frustratingly watched from the driveway. We were told by our mother to hide and be quiet. The officers would say there was nothing they could do if she chose not to answer the door. She rather enjoyed being manipulative and in control. Since Gary would no longer give her that liberty, my father continued to play the role of that victim.

I believe my mother continued her work as a bartender at the Time Warp, the bar where they had met. Little did she know that the bar's name would become a metaphor for her life as she physically aged decades during her time with Gary because of all the physical abuse to her face. I am also fairly certain that her continued employment at the bar is one of the biggest reasons why the fighting lingered on for so long. Gary left his wife and children to be with us. Needless to say, it made for very bitter circumstances in several homes, and you could always feel the tension in the air. My mother would stalk his ex-wife and his previous home, which was conveniently located right next to the bar where they had met. She feared that he was still shacking up with his ex.

I knew everything when it came to her personal life. In fact, I knew way too much. I remember once when we hopped into her green stingray corvette. Gary had gifted her this car soon after moving in. (Not that he could at all afford it.) It was a notable little gesture to lessen the shitstorm that he would unleash on her life, I suppose. She was severely intoxicated, and I never should have gotten into the vehicle with her. She talked to me, as usual, like I was her thirty-year-old best friend, bitching and complaining that she better not find Gary back at his old house.

My mother never once spoke to us or acknowledged us as children. We were tiny adults in her eyes. Even when her grandchildren came later in life, she was incapable of knowing what conversations were appropriate for a young child. We had to hear about everything from the blood clots of her periods to the bills she had to pay. She had no filter, and her mouth gave new meaning to the word *foul*.

As we drove in her corvette, we swayed back and forth across the yellow lines in the center of the road. I could smell the booze on her breath as she barked and complained. It felt no different than any other day, but then it happened. We slid off the road, just missing a tree or two, and we screeched to a stop just inches before plowing through someone's home. I was staring into a giant picture window displaying someone's fucking living room. Three more inches and we would have gone right through it! Thank God nobody was inside to bear witness. And conveniently, there was no one else in the immediate area or on the road to witness what she had just done.

We sat there in shock for a moment. I was sure my little heart would beat right out of my chest cavity. I saw the panic in her eyes, and I feared we could have been dead or at least badly hurt. After a few silent seconds of staring at each other, jaws dropped, she peeled out across their lawn, leaving fresh skid marks in their grass. She steered the car back onto the road and proceeded to drive us back home. I guess we were done stalking for the day. It became yet another moment that would just be erased from her memory, as if it didn't happen. Thankfully, we were blessed to pull safely into our driveway a few minutes later. The shock of car incident must have sobered her up enough to drive straight this time.

This was about the exact time when I would begin to welcome regular visits from Child Protective Services. The intervention took place at my elementary school. I would be pulled from class and told that someone had come to speak with me. As a teacher now, we see this all the time. But back in the '80s, this was a rare occurrence. Jaws dropped and curious minds began inquiring about what was going on when CPS would show up at the school's door.

I had a rather ripe black eye one school day. I remember my teacher asking me what had happened. I very matter-of-factly replied, *My mother hit me in the face.* A little further into the school day, I was escorted out of the room to speak privately with some strange adults in the principal's office. I don't remember what I told them. I don't even recall what pissed her off enough to hit me so hard in the first place. But this would be the first of many visits from various CPS workers and their questioning.

After a couple more unexpected visits from the social workers, my mother was keen on them. She began brainwashing us, telling us that we'd better not talk or tell the truth or that they would take us far away. She concocted any bullshit story she could muster up to scare the shit out of us and save her own ass. And like all unconditionally loving children, we did exactly what she asked of us: We lied for her. We protected her, even though she never had any intention of protecting us. We would remain tight-lipped and pretend we couldn't recall whatever they were asking us. I know many of the subsequent cases were calls that my father had reported himself. Each time we had a visit with him, he learned more and more about the insanity taking place within our walls. I can't imagine how that must have felt as a parent, to know his children were being exposed to such things and have no power other than reporting it to the police or to CPS.

Those reports never seemed to warrant even one ounce of action. I came to learn much later in life that there may have been a good reason for that. A dear neighbor of mine made a confession to me about a time she finally worked up the nerve to call CPS on my mother and Gary. She said the voice on the other end scolded her, asking, "How could you have the nerve to call on your own neighbors?" The CPS worker was local and was also a personal friend of our family. She disregarded the claim after making my neighbor feel awful for her actions. Can you even imagine how many possible other scenarios there may have been just like this? Or perhaps the disappearance of any paper trail of proof? I was beyond disgusted to hear concrete proof of this failure in the system. What grown person, let alone one working for CPS, would think it was okay to ignore the needs and neglect of children?

One evening, we were all home and gathered in the living room. We were plopped around on the furniture watching television to relax just before bedtime. Crazy Gary was a truck driver at that time. He sat in the recliner filling out his paperwork as he always did when he'd return from a truck run. My mother was interrogating him while he worked to fill in the necessary lines. She couldn't stop questioning his whereabouts and time frame. We knew right where this was headed and that my mother wouldn't stop. She was incapable of harmony. Moments of peace were uneasy for her. The argument got heated quickly, as usual. F-bombs and accusations flew around our living room like fireworks! Kids in the room? Who cares? Neither of them could even see us through their tunnel vision of selfishness.

He took his clipboard full of paperwork and whipped it at her to shut her up. His throw was like tossing a frisbee, and it whizzed past our eyes with the force and speed of light. The rounded metal clamp, the part you would pinch with your thumb, was stuck in my mother's head like the tip of an arrowhead. She literally had a fucking clipboard sticking straight up out of her head, standing tall on its own, as it was that deeply embedded into her scalp. We all started screaming, Mother included. He lurched up from his seat to see what he had done, a bit of amusement in his eyes. "Wow, how the fuck did I manage that?" I could hear him say. Blood trickled down into my mother's eyes. He warned her to calm down—as if that were ever going to happen.

Gary then proceeded to yank the clipboard out of her scalp with one strong tug, resulting in even more blood. Head injuries are the worst for bleeding, and this was no exception. It looked equivalent to a scene from *The Shining*. There was absolutely no doubt that she needed stitches for this one, but there was also no chance in hell that she was going to tell the hospital what had just happened. He did his best to clean and bandage the millionth wound he had inflicted upon on her body. She would lie still for the next few days while icing it until it closed enough to begin healing. Thank God for the body's amazing ability to repair itself, as she would be spending many, many years healing the physical trauma on her own.

As I mentioned, Gary was a trucker in the beginning years, so he would be gone for a few days and then be home for a short stretch. When he was in the house with us, tensions were always magnified, and the physical fights were a regular occurrence. My mom always accused him of being unfaithful or lying about where he'd been. Not surprising, considering they started their relationship off as a secret affair. Neither was a stranger to the world of infidelity. My mom's own past actions surely fueled her current paranoia that he was likely being unfaithful to her.

Early in their relationship, we took a car ride to a house where we gathered with my stepfather's family to celebrate his birthday. His mother came forth with a gift for him to open. I watched as she handed it to him, her face beaming with proud motherly love. He opened it for everyone to see. It was a scrapbook album that she had created for him. Having made a few of these myself as an adult, I appreciate the kind of love and effort that goes into such a gift. As she turned the pages, however, I observed that most of the contents were clippings of newspaper articles. *Was he an avid athlete in his early days?* I wondered what this asshole possibly could have achieved in his short lifetime with such a horrific temper and a hatred against women.

I followed up and investigated later that evening at home. When everyone was busy, I mused through the pages his mother had so carefully assembled for him. Turns out, they weren't newspaper articles referring to anything good he had done in the world. Instead, they were archives of all his arrests. I am not joking even slightly when I say it was a vast collection! And she had placed them perfectly in chronological order! *What kind of mother saves this kind of shit?* I wondered. To showcase in a handcrafted album, nonetheless!

Trust me when I say that this gift was not given to be demeaning. She was proud! He was prouder! It was fucking nauseating. There sat the album on our coffee table, sheer proof that he was an actual piece of shit. There were pages and pages of hardcore evidence, yet my mother embraced her life and future with Gary by her side. I could not understand it. I could not make sense of what she saw that I didn't. He wasn't remotely handsome or charming. He was a creep in every sense of the word. He made all of my senses cringe. Clearly, my mother was bona fide nuts. Just like him.

This inner knowing I had of his creepiness would be confirmed many times. It seemed that I could not get away from finding incriminating evidence against him. Another time, I came across an envelope of freshly developed pictures, photographs I wish I'd never laid my eyes on. They unveiled some of my deepest childhood disgust. They also mark the precise pivoting moment that I went from being and feeling like a child, to that of a responsible adult.

The envelope was sitting out on the table. Not even a little bit hidden or disguised. This was back in the '80s when you had to pop a film cartridge into a camera to take pictures. Then you dropped the film off to a pharmacy or a drop box somewhere to have the images developed. Your envelope was usually ready to pick up in about a week. I didn't know who the photos belonged to, but as a naturally curious kid, I flipped open the top and began to skim through them. Let me remind you that I was about eight years old at that point.

I was surprised to find that they were all pictures of my Cabbage Patch dolls! Every single one of them. As I proceeded, my heart sank, and my mind exploded with a plethora of emotions, ranging from sad to mad, rage to disgust, and betrayal. I thought I would literally toss my cookies. *How could they?* My dolls were undressed to appear nude. They were placed in sexual poses, grouped together, portraying a sexual orgy of sorts on my mother's bed. (Don't ask me how I even knew that at such a young age.) Some dolls held our kitchen knives in their lifeless hands. Their poses and positions changed and became more vulgar with each passing image.

I threw the pictures and ran screaming in horror to my mother. *What kind of cruel joke could this be?* These were my baby dolls, my solitude and getaway under the roof of hell, dolls that I loved and cuddled on a daily basis. These toys kept me young and innocent, and these assholes had just tainted their existence in my childhood world. They scarred my image of them for life, and I had photos to freaking prove it! I cried hard, ugly tears. I could not make sense of this. It felt like a personal attack, a punishment of sorts. A robbery of my youth. My mother just laughed. She told me to calm down and that it was *just a joke.*

A joke? What kind of sick, unhealthy adults sat around and posed their child's dolls in derogatory positions? And, what's worse, take photos of these obscene ideas? Who has the actual balls to drop off film containing such vulgarity and then show their faces to claim the photos? My mother and her freak husband, that's who. It was like ripping the Band-Aid off a fresh wound. I could feel the layers of my childhood innocence being taken from me. Why did they insist on making me and my possessions part of their X-rated circus and craziness? Nothing was sacred, not even my cherished toys, for God's sake.

Scars upon scars. This was my life now. Exposed to all things adult, no discretion. I was living in an R-rated movie. I will never understand why they could not see us for the children that we were. Even when party time rolled around at our house, nothing was hidden or kept secret. In between the fighting, they played pretend and invited people over for good times. Family, neighbors, friends—anyone who was up for celebrating with food and booze. When they gathered, they often smoked bongs of marijuana and laughed as they blew smoke into our unsuspecting faces and got us kids high as kites as well. And when they were leaving to go party elsewhere all night, they would kindly chop prescribed Valium pills in half and hand them to us like candy, keeping us calm for the babysitters, of course. Drugs were introduced into my life as just a wee child by my own mother. You know you are "white trash" when your first bout with doing drugs includes your mother as the supplier.

The Gift

> "I am not what happened to me. I am
> what I choose to become." —Carl Jung

Do you remember as a child how you would wish almost every day of your life that you could hurry and grow up already? You dreamed of your own place and a job to make yourself some money, and then you got there and thought to yourself, *What in the actual hell was I thinking?*

I am fairly certain that these thoughts started for me around the age of six. That's about the precise time I began to comprehend the level of dysfunction that ran rabid in my family. All I could think about was getting "out" of this life and into the one I knew at my core was available to me. Something safer. Something loving. Anything other than what I was currently experiencing.

I was required to grow up at a very early age. It was an ugly, forced truth. I was like an adult stuck inside a child's body. I had overseen and overheard entirely too much—so many inappropriate situations and conversations. I knew unthinkable things about the birds and bees and everything in between.

Ironically, this level of maturity would be another one of those saving graces as I proceeded through the doorways of life. This level of maturity gave me unwavering confidence and a sense of boldness that I carry with me still today.

I trusted myself. I trusted my decisions and actions. (If you remove a few wild teenage years from the equation.) I knew things that peers my own age would not even find out about until later in their college days. My adultlike mind helped me navigate through some rocky years of adolescence, making decisions as the "future Margo" would want to live, and not going off the deep end like many of my squirrely teenage friends did at the time.

I spent a good majority of my adolescence with a straight head, a sound mind, and my eyes steady on the promising future. A ticket out.

you ARE **not** REQUIRED TO **SET** yourself ON FIRE TO KEEP others WARM

—*Unknown*

CHAPTER 6

Suitcases

AS I MENTIONED, THIS LIFE of mine was stuck on repeat. My siblings and I were growing older, but the happenings in our home remained predictably the same. Police visits and bloody fights were so normal and routine that it felt like the world stopped caring and ignored us, turning a blind eye to our continued suffering. Eventually, police units took longer and longer to respond to calls, and I even remember a time or two when they didn't bother to show up at all.

I spent as much time as I possibly could hanging out away from home. I overstayed my welcome at friends' houses on a daily basis. Thankfully, one of my best friends in high school lived just around the corner, and I made myself at home there as if I was part of the family. While I think it took a toll on her parents, they were certainly forgiving, as they too knew what was happening at my house and they never asked me to leave.

By this time, my mother and Gary began wearing out ties with our family members. My aunts and uncles, who used to be quite close with us, stayed away, avoiding the toxicity whenever possible. But my grandparents always seemed to be right there, rescuing my mother every time she cried wolf. I sadly remember an incident when they were inadvertently lured into Mom and Gary's violent ritual.

We must have been having a family dinner or celebration of sorts. Gatherings always meant an abundance of booze or beer, and this evening was no different. My grandparents drank pretty heavily too. Beverages were flowing steadily, and so was my mother's mouth. And when she started to get louder and louder, Gary would show up to the fighting ring as well. The adults were all in the kitchen. It was only a matter of time before fists were clenched and arms were swinging. Even with my grandparents in the room, Gary and my mom would carry on in such a way. My grandparents tried to separate their bodies, but it was impossible to intervene. Their sickness and need to physically hurt one another would stop for no one. I watched my poor grandparents add to the fury, hitting Gary, trying to divert his attention from destroying my mom's face. That's when I saw my grandmother reach for the cast-iron skillet on the stovetop. Thankfully, the grease in it was not heated. She whacked that son of a bitch so hard on the back of his head that I was sure his brains exploded.

Unfortunately, they did not. But the hit was hard enough to drop that psycho to the floor with a thunderous thud. There was no blood, but he was knocked out for at least a few counts. The kitchen walls and floors glistened with grease splatter. I could not freaking believe this monster had the balls to lash out at my elderly grandparents! He was a real gem. I can't even say that I lost more respect for those two idiots because that was already long, long gone.

You'd think maybe this would be an eye-opener, the revelation she needed to finally realize what her choices were costing her. But as I said before, my mother had blinders on. She refused to think or feel for anyone but her own damn self. I was growing so tired of this dreadful home life. *Couldn't we just pretend to enjoy each other's company for one single day?*

I am not sure why I thought it would be a good idea to plan something for my upcoming birthday. I would be turning eleven, even though I was already living the life of a twenty-year-old. I wanted so badly to feel like a normal kid if even for just one day. My special day. My mother agreed to let me plan a slumber party. I would invite five or six girls from school to stay the night. I knew this was a gamble, considering everyone and their mother knew our household history. To this day, I am convinced these mothers phoned each other and banded together to make a special day happen for me. I could not believe they were actually coming!

The girls began arriving and the fun soon followed. I remember coloring and making Shrinky Dinks in our kitchen oven. We giggled and gossiped and enjoyed each other's company. We planned to camp out on the living room floor where all the pillows and sleeping bags were arranged for our secret all-nighter!

I wish I could say my mother was smart enough to plan this party when the asshole wouldn't be home. But for some reason, plans changed, and he was there. I prayed he would behave himself. More importantly, I prayed that my mother, for one day, would just play the role of my mother by controlling her mouth and outlandish behavior. *Why did I ever think that would be the case?* Little did I know, this would turn out to be one of the worst nights yet! Yes, there was always more to come.

It started as all the girls and I laid around chatting and laughing in the living room. I could hear the bickering from behind closed doors. I guess I should give them an ounce of credit for at least initially trying to keep it down. But as you can imagine, things began to escalate rather fast. Soon, he was hitting her, and my friends heard every bit of it. They were frightened beyond belief. A couple of them raced straight to the phone to call their parents to come and get them. I was mortified, embarrassed beyond belief! Their parents said they would be right there to pick them up, but I did not want my party to end. I went from embarrassed to furious. My blood boiled.

I had to intervene. I began yelling at my mom and Looney Gary, like an adult scolding a naughty little child with a pointed finger. "Stop it! Knock this off right now! You are scaring my friends! How could you?" As usual, no one heard my words. I was once again invisible. My friends huddled together in disbelief. They were petrified, truly petrified. Little did they know that this was my daily way of life. It was thoroughly exhausting to be so unwanted or cared about.

We waited in the porch area for the first set of parents to arrive. The next thing we knew, Gary was dragging my mom across the living room by her head. The weight of her body tried hard to stay on the ground and break away from his hold. Their flailing bodies wrestled right across every neatly positioned blanket and pillow. She had nothing against his manpower even if she was fierce herself. He was like a maniac when things got this heated, and there was no defusing him. He dragged my mother out the front door by the hair on her head, down the steps, and into his truck. She cried and pleaded for help. I am sure the neighbors phoned the police from all the screaming at that point, but I chose to call as well, just in case. The truck peeled out of the driveway, racing down our street at full speed.

The police arrived just as a couple sets of parents pulled up. I was trying to give a report to the officer while also mourning the fact that my friends were leaving one by one. Tears poured relentlessly down my birthday cheeks. The adults helped to contact the remaining parents, and all I could think about was how I would never have a friend in life again. It was humiliating. Surely they would all regret feeling sorry for me in the first place and allowing their kids to be part of potential danger. I thought my life was over.

The next twelve hours or so did not get any better. A couple of officers stayed to take the report and to see that the other children were safely picked up. Several other cop cars were dispatched to search for the whereabouts of the truck containing my already beaten mother. Luckily, the search didn't take too long. It's almost as if they knew his favorite spots and just where to look by then. What they found minutes later would land itself on the front page of the paper the following day.

I cannot recall specific details, but it went something like this: he drove my mother to a vineyard, a field filled with rows and rows of grapes. Even though we lived in a small city, it was surrounded by lots of country roads with lush land for farming. Grapes grow in abundance in our part of New York and are quite the welcoming aroma during their harvest in the fall. For some reason, there was construction going on at this particular site that summer. Gary more than likely knew that because he was often hired "under the table" to operate a backhoe on local projects. I am guessing that the coffin-sized hole in the ground they found my mother lying in was intentional. A carefully premeditated plan thought out by a sick, psychotic man.

In his usual Houdini style, he disappeared without a trace as sirens drew near. Did he plan to bury her alive? Did he think she was dead as he plopped her tattered body down into the gaping hole in the earth? I guess we will never know, and it does not really matter anyhow. Because, as you have likely guessed, she dropped all charges against him. Just like she had every single other time. Nowadays, you would never get away with that. But back then, it was allowed. Happy birthday to me. Another wonderful childhood memory to add to all the joyous others.

You might be wondering how this was even possible, that we children had not been taken away from her. I always wondered that too. Times were so different back then. Mothers had all the rights. Even with all the police visits and endless calls to Child Protective Services, my father could not convince the law to give him custody. Talk about a fucked-up, failed system. Some of my childhood could have actually been salvaged if they had removed us at the onset of this turmoil. Instead, I spent years and years being forced to watch, up close and personal.

Life under this dreaded roof did eventually come to an abrupt end—at least for my older brother and me. We were about to embark on yet another "after school surprise." As we got closer to our house, we noticed stacked items on the porch and the steps. Bags and boxes, to be specific. I can remember feeling my footsteps slow down, as if I were walking through drying glue. My mind was stopping my body from physically moving forward. I felt my breath cease as my mind flooded with memories of the great Florida move a couple years earlier. *Were we moving again? What was going on here? What was this stuff? And why was my mom standing outside waiting for us?*

Turns out, this would be the day my mother would let us go. Her husband had ordered her to kick my older brother and me out of the house. It was him or us; she had to choose. And she made the choice rather easily, I might add. Did she tell us this as young children? Yep. She told us exactly what was going on: "You are going to live with your father. I packed up all your shit. Call your dad and tell him to come get you guys."

We waited for our ride outside on the steps. Suddenly our life in the house of horrors was ending. I was in disbelief. I didn't know whether to cry or to sing from the rooftops. I couldn't, however, stop thinking about my little brother. Why was he being forced to remain in the gates of hell? Oh, that's right—perhaps it was because my dad was not his biological father. It wasn't ever discussed out loud, though everyone knew the facts. Hell, we could all have different biological fathers considering her promiscuous lifestyle. Her guilt in knowing the truth for certain with my little brother made her keep him there with her. Unfortunately, he would be exposed to even more mayhem in the years to come. I would only get to see him on weekends or at school from that point on. I had been his caretaker and mother figure for all those years leading up to this moment. I had raised that boy. Consequently, I had to live with the guilt that we were free and he was still imprisoned in a house of horrors.

My older brother opted to live with my grandparents, who weren't that far away. I moved in with my father and stepmother. She had four children from her previous marriage, all living in the house. This meant there wasn't much room. Not to mention the challenges of trying to blend a family. It was fairly short-lived. I believe I lived at my dad's for about a year or so before that season of my life also came to an end.

The Gift

> "You're not required to set yourself
> on fire to keep other people warm."
> —Author unknown

As if transitioning into adolescence wasn't hard enough, I was pretty much forced to navigate and find my "space" in the world at that point in my life. I knew I didn't want to remain with my mother and her crazy lifestyle. But I didn't exactly fit in with my father's new family either. I was already falling in love with my now husband, but we were certainly too young to start our lives together.

This whirlwind of change once again forced me to spend a lot of time turning inward. Would I let another obstacle forever label me as a victim of circumstance? Not a chance. My sense of self-worth was growing stronger by the day. These people did not define me. These households did not define me. These roots did not define me, either. I would not let them. There would be no bowing down to play victim to circumstance.

I knew I was worthy. Lovable. Hell, I was even fun and enjoyable. Regrettably, neither of my parents ever took the time to figure that out about me. But their opinion of me, or the lack thereof, would not be the cause of my demise. As far as I was concerned, they missed out. It was their loss. Instead, their neglect became my fuel for loving myself more. I was able to exit stage right with my magic potion of self-worth, value-sized! This was something no one was ever going to take from me. I always knew I was better than any of the things that happened to me.

THE *child*
WHO is NOT

EMBRACED

by *the* village

WILL BURN IT

down **to** *feel*
it's

WARMTH

—*African Proverb*

CHAPTER 7

It Takes a Village

HAVE YOU IDENTIFIED THE BROKEN, failed system yet? At this point in my story, it's only natural to wonder how the three of us children were repeatedly left inside the walls of that chaotic home for way too many years. Worse, my youngest brother was still stuck there. How did those grown-ups sleep at night, just walking away after each investigation? How could a man who led such a corrupt and criminal life be free to walk the streets so effortlessly and proud? Where was the system when it came to identifying and incarcerating predators who beat women and ruined families? Sadly, we weren't the only household that would fall victim to his undoing. There were others before us, and there would be others after us.

I use zero exaggeration when I say the police department and children's services were called likely more than a hundred times—if not by my own father, then by neighbors or the school district. Never once were we forcibly removed from her home that I can recall, even though our own father, who we visited on the weekends, was a viable option just down the road. I was never granted that feeling of rescue that I so very much longed for.

Despite my aggravation and disappointment in the failed system back then, I thank my lucky stars for the village of neighborhood support that quite literally helped to raise us kids— one of the true benefits of residing in Small Town, USA. You almost couldn't help but look after one another. The houses were so close that they may as well have been connected. Only a few feet of space separated each tiny two-story unit on our block. The roadway that separated us from the houses across the street was also narrow. Traffic was never too busy on our side street, and we often played out in the road. Tiny corner bars could be found at both ends of our short street. They were usually a side-hustle business latched right onto someone's actual household. In my earliest days, I remember my grandfather frequented both. Occasionally, I would pop in to see him if I spotted his car parked nearby. He'd give me quarters for the jukebox and then let me pretend to be a rockstar while knocking balls into the pool table. This was only if the bar was lacking patrons and the old timers could use a little entertainment, of course.

Once, when I was just a small child, I decided to ride my tricycle down the street stark naked. (When I was very little, I couldn't bear to keep clothes on my body.) A neighbor across the street noticed me taking off without warning. I was clearly too young to be hightailing it on my own, so he chased after me, yelling my name out loud. He eventually caught up, scooped me up, and proceeded to my doorstep with a naked kiddo in one hand and a tricycle in the other.

It was such a different time back then. The world was a much-safer and trusted place. Nature was the primary playground for every kid, as electronic devices hadn't surfaced yet. We played in all the streets, yards, and parks that surrounded the houses in our neighborhoods. Every single day, we were out there interacting and playing from sunup 'til sundown. We did not report home until the streetlamps turned on, signaling it was getting late. We would be on our bikes for hours and no one would panic or search for us. There were so many options for us to congregate as large groups, and that is just what we did.

We had an impressive outdoor community pool in our little city. In the summertime, it would cost a couple of coins to spend the entire day there splashing, swimming, and cooling off. Parents were optional, and most of the time it was just packed with us kids. The lifeguards were like glorified babysitters. They kept us all from drowning. They patched up our scrapes and cuts when we fell on the concrete, and they quickly mended our relationships when they saw us in quarrels with our besties over something silly.

Our little city borders the great Lake Erie. So, our tiny beach shores were lined with lifeguards as well. They all played a hand in raising my generation. Whistles blew when we got out of hand or didn't adhere to water rules. And we knew better than to misbehave, as this was a privilege we did not want revoked. The beach was also our playground all summer long and was only a few short blocks away from our front doorstep. We respected that waterfront property as well as those in charge of watching over it.

When I was about eleven or twelve years old, I was hit in the head with a rock while swimming in the lake with friends. Some random jerk was throwing stones from the shore. The lifeguard, who later ended up becoming my brother-in-law, had to bandage up my head like a mummy while we waited for the ambulance to arrive and take over. Luckily, it was just a puncture wound with lots of blood and nothing that required sutures. I still remember the ambulance loading me up to give me a ride home. Nobody was around when we got there. There were no cell phones to call and report the situation. I told them I would be just fine and that they were free to go, so they did. Can you even imagine that scenario going down today? No way!

Just like our time spent at the beach and pool, our surrounding neighborhood streets were equally as safe to roam. My particular street had some of the most compassionate residents you could ask for. These folks knew damn well what was going on in our crazy house. Hell, I am sure they could hear most of it loud and clear. They were the ones who called the police when World War III broke out on any given day. Sadly, I think they also succumbed to the decline in worry and urgency as time went on. I cannot say I blame them. The calls were useless since my mom and Looney Gary would deny everything. We were, of course, instructed to lie about the incidents, and her refusal to cooperate would cause them to turn and walk away.

Couldn't they see the invisible signs we were holding? The ones we held up every time they showed up to our front door. Signs that read, *Help me!* or *Please don't leave me here again!* My body would shake with worry and an instant urge to pee each time they pulled away, because I knew their uninvited presence had just pissed off Gary ten times more than he already was.

I would continue to find respite among the people in the neighboring houses. Thank God these wonderful souls were sympathetic to our troubles. They often fed us, entertained us, and even included us kids in their family outings when they could. I was thankful to have these options as a child. They were a getaway. A glimpse into what "normal" looked and felt like, even if it was just a borrowed feeling for a short time on a given day. I mentally took notes along the way. *This. Someday I will have this. Someday I will make this kind of home and family for myself.* I meant it with conviction and pinky swore with myself to make it come true, no matter what.

Sometimes we even slept out at our neighbors' houses. We had several elderly neighbors who acted much like surrogate grandparents. They often shared their baked goods and desserts with us. They spent a fair amount of time looking after us as we darted through their yards each day. Yards had no boundaries back then. Occasionally, they would even host sleepover movie nights, a place to go for safekeeping and a break from the bitching, bickering, and smashing happening regularly in my home. There were a good handful of younger families residing on our street as well, some of which had children close to our ages. They always went the extra mile to include us kids for picnics, parties, or outings when they could. If we fit in the car, they squeezed us in.

Even the firefighters living in the station through our backyard provided refuge for us on occasion. They warmly welcomed us annoying little kids any time we drove up on our bicycles to their wide-opened garage doors. They would tour us around and occasionally treat us to a twenty-five-cent bottled pop from their Coke machine. They knew. Everyone knew. We were *those* kids. The poor little ones from the house of horror on Downing Lane.

Many thoughts of gratitude go out to the tolerant firefighters at the station and the countless other neighbors who held compassion or space for us children in any way. I pray that all neighborhoods near and far are blessed with these same types of humans extending their kindnesses.

The Gift

"The child that is not embraced by
the village will burn it down to feel
its warmth." —African proverb

I have always held love for my family, despite their shortcomings, and I always will. However, by this particular point in my life, I knew beyond a shadow of a doubt there was no truth to the saying that blood is thicker than water.

As a young girl, I relied heavily on neighbors, friends, and teachers to get me through and to morally support me and hold space for me to be me. To listen when I needed ears. To host a sleepover when I did not want to go home that night or even that weekend. My friends' parents often took me under their wings, knowing that I was safer and better off under their roofs. I learned exceedingly early that family becomes the people you choose to surround yourself with. Family is not always about blood. It is about the people in your life who treat you with respect, accept you, and notice you. They were my "village." My family. My infrastructure.

To this day, I cannot stand when someone hastily uses words like, "But she's your mother." Or "But that is your family." I call bullshit! We have absolutely no obligation to remain in toxic environments or situations. I, myself, participated in one for far too long. Sometimes it means removing ourselves from people we are close to and love, regardless of whether or not they gave birth to us.

I learned so much about networking and finding the people I wanted to have in my corner—those who shared mutual respect. There would be no settling for one-sided love in my life, only relationships that were nurturing, fulfilling, and purposeful were now welcome. I am grateful for this village of others that surrounded me in those dark, unpredictable years of my life. That village was my own personal survival kit, my "toolbox" of humans who I would rely on for escaping my reality. As an adult, I will never forget their generosity and thoughtfulness. They are my supporting roots.

I am proud to say that when searching for an apartment or a house, my criteria will always be based on finding a neighborhood that mimics the one I had as a child—one where neighbors are more like family. A network of people genuinely looking out for the best interests of each other. Ones that could hear my cries or screams if I ever needed them to come to my rescue. Ones that would open their doors for a visit just because ...

As I write this book, I can say that I am lucky enough to have found exactly that in this home where I have raised my own children and family for the past twenty years.

HEROISM doesn't always HAPPEN in a

burst of glory

Sometimes small TRIUMPHS and LARGE hearts CHANGE

THE course of history

—Mary Roach

CHAPTER 8

Sweet Mother Mary

I WAS THIRTEEN WHEN MY paternal grandfather passed away. His death took quite a toll on my grandmother, who played the nurse throughout his illness. He withered away for a long time, and she worked hard tending to all his needs. When he finally perished in the veterans' hospital, I am certain her tired body must have felt instant relief.

She was, by far, the most constant, loving, and nurturing person in my life. Maybe one of the only ones. My grandma was my own personal hero and cheerleader all wrapped up in one. She was the mother and father figure that inspired me to be the person I am today. I hope she will always know how eternally grateful I am that she was chosen to be my person, my saint, my savior in a life of utter chaos.

Any time I spent with my grandma was cherished, calm, and more than welcomed. I would go there as often as possible for visits as a young child. She rescued us three kids many times from the mayhem. I remember secretly dialing her number on the rotary phone. I'd whisper to her that we were grounded and ask if she could please call the house to tell my parents that she needed us to do some chores outside for her. She would willingly oblige, of course. Thankfully, my parents would fall for it and deliver us to her beck and call every time.

There are so many things from my early years that are difficult for me to recall. I imagine that is rightfully so since so much of it is tainted and gruesome. But my grandmother and her home are not part of my foggy brain. I remember every detail about her and that house without fail. I remember the smell of her dogs as you entered the stale hallway of her two-family entrance, the smell of lilacs that adorned her "alley," as she would call it—a tiny courtyard of sorts on the side of the house. I remember the smell of cigarettes in her bathroom or bedroom, which were the only two places she would sneak to have a quick smoke in private. I remember the taste of her overly sweetened coffee that she would let me sip. I remember the sound of the swinging side door opening and closing as the dogs tramped in and out of the house at their will and the squeaking sound of her metal bed mattress as I jumped on and off and on again to lie with her a billion times throughout our visit. I spent as much time by her side as I could when I was a little girl. She had the purest, most gentle nature about her. I don't think I ever once witnessed her being mad. My grandma was quiet and soft-spoken, quite opposite of my big personality. She only ever wanted to please anyone she encountered. She didn't complain—not one single time that I can recall. She was a saint, so tolerant and patient. And while she outwardly no longer partook much in her latest years, she was a devout Catholic in her upbringing. I will never forget her Irish smile; smooth, fair skin; and piercing blue eyes.

I knew that since my grandfather was now gone, my grandmother truly would need help around the house. My older brother had already been living there for a while. He removed himself from all the chaos even sooner than I had the opportunity to. Don't get me wrong—my dad's house was a better option than my mother's by far, but it was tiny. And with our recently acquired stepfamily of four stepbrothers and sisters, it made for tense, tight accommodations.

I was turning fourteen years old when I officially joined my older brother and moved in with my grandmother, who was now widowed. I grabbed a tiny room in the back of her house and turned it into a makeshift teen bedroom as best I could. I remember she crafted a mirrored vanity table of sorts, complete with a bench. You could clearly see her excitement in having me with her full time. I was in middle school then, and the school building was located just a few blocks away from her house. This would be much closer than the long walk I had to make from my Dad's place. It was also conveniently located just down the street from my new boyfriend. I guess it would be fair to say that I had some selfish, hormonal motivation behind the desire to move in as well. But to my defense, she provided more stability for me than anyone else in my life. She always played the role of my caregiver. (And a bonus, who knew I was embarking on the start of my "happily ever after" at the ripe age of fourteen!)

A mutual friend had introduced me to one of the "cool guys" from high school. This guy had a popular yard and garage that I'd only heard about from others. When he drove up on his BMX bike to introduce himself and ask my cousin Heather and me to come hang out with him and his friend, it was a no-brainer that we would take the bait. Picture the movie *Goonies*. He was the Corey Feldman of the pack, a tad rough around the edges, but witty and cute, nonetheless. I wasn't interested whatsoever in acquiring him as a boyfriend at the time. I was, however, looking for an "in" to the cool crowd he was chumming with. He was not necessarily my type, but after a few more invites to hang out, chemistry began to take over and I soon found myself undeniably attracted and wooed by his boyish charm. How convenient that we'd be living in such close proximity through our years of dating and courtship during high school.

I had already spent a good deal of my time hovering around my grandmother's neighborhood anyhow. Most of the friends I spent time with all the lived nearby. We patrolled that neighborhood religiously in those days, back when there was no fear or danger in the streets to the extent there is today. We spent all of our leisure time out in nature then, riding bikes, hanging in parks, or partying in garages.

I should go on record as saying that we were not normal fourteen or fifteen-year-old kids. We were babies who had adult bodies and minds. No exaggeration here. We acted, talked, and looked like we were experienced middle-aged rock stars. Invincible. We stayed up all hours of the night. We snuck out many nights when grownups believed we were fast asleep in our beds. I didn't have to worry about my brother "narking" on me, as he was just two years older and pretty much going through the same adolescent stage as me. He and his "beer brothers" brood were usually partying it up in my grandmother's garage while I strolled down a couple blocks to hang in my future husband's garage. My brother and I had some mutual friends, but for the most part we managed to stay out of each other's hair.

My new boyfriend (now hubby) was a member of a high school version of a fraternity. It was a brotherhood that started even before the college years arrived. My dad had belonged to the same one when he attended our high school decades earlier. This means we attended "kegger" parties in the woods every weekend without fail. Occasionally, we would witness the "pledgees" get paddled-in and accepted. (That would be the day; I would never let someone spank me with a slab of wood in order to belong!) When the weather was bad or too cold, we would pack like sardines into my boyfriend's tiny garage. Body heat and a mini wood stove would do the trick to warm us up. It was either that or the abundance of alcohol we consumed to prove just how cool we were. It didn't seem to matter what crowd you spent your time with; everyone partied at a young age in those days. *Did I mention we were daring, crazy teens?*

I did not give it any thought back then, but now I feel awful that my grandma had to deal with me in those awkward, overconfident teen years. I was such a know-it-all! (Much like my own daughters today!) I am sure my every action kept her on her toes, worrying. Adolescents have much less fear than adults. It is common to flirt with danger and feel invincible. To be honest, my friends and I are lucky to be alive. No, really, we are. We did way too many stupid things at such a young age, too many to mention or confess here. Perhaps in another time and a different book. It's bittersweet when I look back on it all. I'm not sure what the actual hell we were thinking. To say we were daring would be an understatement.

I'd be a liar if I didn't say I was glad to have gotten it all out of my system at a young age, before heading to college, where I got seriously focused and did quite well. But being so careless and experimental at such a young age comes with a cost. It fast-forwarded my mental age by at least ten years. And let's not forget, I had already been robbed of my earliest years. I never really had the chance to be a kid. I went right from shielding myself from a life of continuous domestic violence to falling in love and escaping all of it, from toddler to adult in the blink of an eye. There was never any in-between. I missed those years entirely. Like a flash of lightning, they passed me right on by. And even though I will tell the story saying I felt "grown up" at around age thirteen, that would be an exaggeration. I really grew up at around age six or seven when I first began caring for my emotional needs and turning inward to pray for the safety of myself and my brothers. That was back when we siblings were first exposed to things no child should ever have to witness.

It wasn't long after moving in with my grandma that I legally emancipated myself from my parents. I didn't speak to my mom much at all, and I had an estranged relationship with my dad at that point too. Successful stepfamilies are a rare occurrence, and we were no exception. My dad was still drinking heavily at this time, and we had an incident where he lashed out at me in rage. It didn't get physical, but it was just moments from occurring. I remember he called me my mother's name and told me I was exactly like her. The intensity of the moment took me back to the whole broken leg episode from a decade before. Hearing him say her name to me would create an even bigger divide in our already-lacking father-daughter relationship.

I had actual court documentation to solidify this split from my parents, and my grandmother cared for me full time now that I was legally independent of my parents. Even though my Dad was still ordered to keep me under his health insurance, my grandmother was now my caretaker as far as the State of New York was concerned. Her elderly one-person income was slim to none, so I naturally qualified for public assistance or welfare. I was able to redeem the monthly benefit payouts myself, as I was, in a sense, considered an adult then. The monthly payments were miniscule in size, but were obviously helpful to a broke teenaged girl finding her way.

I'll never know how my grandma felt about inadvertently landing herself in a primary parenting role. We went from cuddling and baking together to the need for laying ground rules for curfews and other cautions. This obviously changed the dynamic in our relationship to some degree. Teenagers are not the most cooperative or compassionate people on earth. (Or, at least, not in my case.) When I wasn't working or going to school, I wanted to be gone with my friends doing God only knows what! We would barely see each other throughout the day when she could have used my help more than ever. I always had an excuse for needing to be elsewhere with friends. You know how it is: those teenage priorities got the best of me.

Once, I came home to tell her about the upcoming spring break trip I would soon be taking with my three best friends. God bless her soul. I was only sixteen and a junior in high school, mind you. We bought round-trip Greyhound bus tickets to Myrtle Beach from our little town in western New York. We wired a deposit to a cheap two-story motel, which we booked for a full two weeks directly on the shore. She thought we were nuts, and she was absolutely correct. We felt invincible, as if we could do whatever the hell we wanted. I still don't know how on earth we convinced the other three sets of parents to allow us to go.

Personally, I had leverage to plead my own case. My soldier boyfriend was stationed just an hour away from where we would be vacationing. I think this at least gave my grandmother an ounce of relief. She knew a good deal of my time there would be spent catching up with my soldier boy. She also knew that, any time I got an idea in my head, there was simply no stopping me. She reminded me of this character trait often.

Needless to say, we survived that trip. Four crazy young girls, two dreadfully long voyages on the Greyhound bus lines, and two long weeks of living out of a chintzy beachfront motel room where we cooked SpaghettiOs's for dinner on our hot plate. Lots of stories to tell from this epic trip! But that would likely be a whole other book as well.

The Gift

> "Heroism doesn't always happen in
> a burst of glory. Sometimes small
> triumphs and large hearts change the
> course of history." —Mary Roach

Many people, especially when they are young, think of heroes as superhuman beings that only exist in cartoons, movies, or perhaps in the Bible. There is an ideology that heroes must be creatures who are larger than life, or they must have at least conquered large-than-life obstacles.

My sweet grandma was the first person who truly made me understand that heroism resides in all humans and in everyday people like her and like me. It's self-respect and self-loyalty. It's courage and ambition. It's the willingness to try without being afraid to put yourself out there. Being a hero is risk-taking and vulnerability at its very core; it's a badge of honor we are gifted, if only we are willing to discover our true capabilities.

She had been my rock and hero for all those crazy years, but what she was really teaching me was to be my own hero. To save myself. She would often share with me that her biggest regret in life was relying on others. She wished she had done more for herself. She hated feeling dependent. She had never even obtained a license to drive a vehicle and was therefore always waiting on others to take her where she needed to go.

My grandma would always say things to me, such as, "There is no stopping you, Margo. You make up your mind, and that is all there is to it." I did not realize at the time that she was living vicariously through my every action. She beamed as I conquered each chapter in my life and rose above the hellish bullshit I had been forced to tolerate as a child. She is the exact reason I vowed to become my very own heroine, one of the most valuable lessons a human can achieve in their lifetime here on earth. Here I was in my late teens, knowing without hesitation that I could do whatever I put my mind to. Period.

Heroes not only save others; they stand up and save themselves.

YOU *can't* go BACK and CHANGE THE BEGINNING but *you* can START WHERE *you are* and CHANGE *the* *ending*

— C. S. Lewis

PART II

Lessons in Adulting

CHAPTER 9

Time for Me to Fly

MY FIRST LOVE REALLY WAS the "cool kid" on the block back then. As I mentioned, he lived just up the street, holding weekend hangouts in his garage. I'll spare you the happenings between those four walls because that is not what this book is about. The important thing to note is that my intuition served me well back then. I knew this kid would someday be my happily ever after, even if he did break up with my controlling teenage self a time (or ten). I was a clingy girlfriend, and often he just wanted to hang with the boys. But something in me could foresee our future. I knew it in my core without any shadow of a doubt. We'd marry and create a family and a life together someday.

He wasn't just my boyfriend. He was my best friend and confidant from the start. He was my go-to. He knew every detail of my shitastic life—and still loved and accepted me for me. (Well, at least most of the time.) He was the kind of boyfriend that would give my seventy-year-old grandmother a ride to the store because I was still too young to drive. He was the kind of boyfriend who would polish my toes and let me perm his hair. We just clicked. Our bond was strong from day one—stronger than we even knew at the time. He and I have been together for all but the first thirteen years of my life. To call him my husband seems like an understatement of sorts. He is my partner in life. My better half.

If you were to ask me who the most influential people in my life have been, he would be tied with my grandmother in first place. Like my grandmother, he has always been my biggest cheerleader—back then, and still now, to this day. He is one of the most complacent, calm, well-rounded, and giving people I know. He would do anything for anyone. It's a bonus that he can cry over a sad movie or a good poem without feeling ashamed or too manly to show it. He's a real keeper. The best part is that he has always believed in me. No matter what crazy idea I sprang forward with, he has encouraged me to follow it through and see what happens. When I achieve results, he is the first to acknowledge my hard work and determination. When it doesn't work out, he is the first to remind me that at least I had the gusto to try.

We were, by no means, innocent children back then. We were constantly pushing the envelope as teens. But I wouldn't trade a single second of that, either. Like everything else I had already been through, these times shaped the people we turned out to be today. And for that, I am proud. Naturally, I have remorse for the things I did as a teen while living under my grandmother's roof. (Most of which she had not a clue about.) But I know with certainty that she would forgive me. She knows, just as much as I do, that it was all part of the big plan and that those experiences were a necessary part of my evolution. I know I make her proud every day. I know she is with me, cheering me on all the while.

I spent a good deal of my time up the street at his house. Every morning before school started, I darted up the street to wake him for the day. I probably overstayed my welcome, as I always wanted to be near him. He was a pretty popular guy, after all, with tons of friends, so there was never a dull moment surrounding him. I didn't want to miss out on a thing.

On the day I turned sixteen, I got my first job at a local fast-food chain. Part-time hours and schoolwork kept me rather busy. This was the best thing for me since my guy would soon be leaving to serve in the military for the next couple of years. He was set to graduate high school at seventeen. I still had three years of high school left, resulting from a setback I brought upon myself when I failed the seventh grade and had to repeat the year. I hadn't taken school seriously in my early adolescence. The period of time when he was away serving allowed me to clean up my act. I started to work earnestly on school studies and my future. I improved my attitude and my grades. I felt I had already tested most of my limits from ages thirteen to sixteen, so much of my curiosity and ignorance was behind me. Most of it, anyway. I still had a few adventures left in me.

Because I was receiving financial help from the government, I also had "working requirements." I held a part-time job already, but I gladly accepted the opportunity to be a secretarial assistant when a temporary position opened at an office not too far from my gram's. It was the summer just before my senior year rolled around. I clocked in each morning and worked alongside a much older woman who ran a little agency that helped displaced women get back on their feet. She took me under her wing and was a delight to be around. She had a grandmotherly type vibe about her, and she patiently taught me how to do tasks I had never completed before.

One morning, she came to work rather late and visibly distraught. Turned out, a couple of local teens had stolen her car and then wrapped it around a telephone pole during a chase with the police. She confessed that she had left the keys in the car, and she was angry with herself. I did my best to offer her my ear. You can imagine my surprise when I learned later that evening that it was my youngest brother, who was fourteen years old then, and two of his friends who had stolen her car. I felt sick to my stomach. *How could this possibly be happening?* My roots had a way of resurfacing every now and then. I didn't even see my brother much in those days. There was no way he knew that she and I were connected in any way.

I would learn later that choosing her car was completely random and coincidental. That did not, however, soften the blow. When she heard my brother's name, she immediately came to me with accusations. Why wouldn't she? I had to explain my way out of this turmoil with my head hanging low in utter embarrassment. *I need to get the fuck out of this town*, I thought. My little brother would be shipped off to a juvenile detention center on the other side of the state for stealing my boss's car and totaling it, but I was served a sentence as well: I had to continue showing up to work each day next to a woman who no longer trusted or valued me. Thankfully, there were only a couple of weeks left of this job. How horribly awkward those remaining days were. You cannot make this stuff up.

Before I knew it, I was ready to graduate high school. Those years gave true meaning to the phrase "Time flies when you're having fun!" I was just about eighteen years old. I planned to move away in the fall for college. My guy and I mailed love letters back and forth. I remember kissing the envelopes with bright lipstick before sending them on their way to his base down south. He would want to kill me because, to embarrass him, the sergeant who handed out the mail would make him drop down and kiss the envelope while doing pushups. I thought it was rather entertaining. Even with miles between us, we spoke of our future together and began to think about what was to come.

I was barely on speaking terms with my mother and am not sure why I foolishly decided to tap into her as a resource while planning my own graduation party at a local picnic spot. My mother was actually a rather seasoned cook and caterer. She was set to make most of the food for the party (if I paid for it), and I would handle the decorations and details. Of course, I should have known better than to rely on my so-called mother for anything that important in my life. But, as usual, I wanted to give her a chance for redemption.

Just after graduation and only a week before my party, I found my grown mother with a neck full of dark and visible "hickeys." I was mortified and embarrassed to say the least. *Seriously? Did she think she was fifteen? Yuck.* My gut instinct and further investigation would lead me to confirm that her psycho blast from the past had resurfaced. It seemed that my woman-beating ex-stepfather had been the one who planted them there. After a few years of finally ridding herself of him, he intentionally left a bloodstained sign to let us all know he was back. Gary had ditched my mother to prey on another vulnerable woman and her family. Although they did divorce, he occasionally reemerged to play mind games with my willing and unstable mother. My instant disgust in her led us into a screaming match. Needless to say, the heated argument ended with her telling me to fuck off and mind my own business. Oh, and to throw my own fucking grad party! Alrighty then. Guess I should have seen that one coming.

I borrowed somewhere around $600 from my lifesaving grandmother. Mind you, she hardly ever left her house, and she had no plans to actually attend the party herself. But she did want to make sure that I still had my celebration despite my mother pulling the rug out from under me yet again. She was on a fixed income and could not afford to fork over that kind of money. So I promised to replace 100 percent of it with the proceeds from my graduation cards. I then had to scramble to find last-minute food options. I shopped carefully and was able to purchase some party trays of finger foods, a keg of beer, and minimal decorations to make it all happen.

Much to my surprise, no one except close high school friends showed up that day. I couldn't understand why this was happening. We still had a large amount of family living nearby, and many neighbors we were close with, many of which had RSVP'd to attend. The guest list was nearly a hundred people! After panicking and making a few phone calls to aunts and cousins, I learned that my loving mother had called everyone just days before to tell them my party was cancelled and that it would no longer happen.

That rotten, no-good mother of mine had sabotaged my life once again, knowing full well that my party would be planned to carry on without her. She knew my grandmother would save the day as usual. She cancelled out of pure spite because that's how she operated. To this day, she is the most vindictive and cruel person I have ever met. If she couldn't be there to celebrate and make some claim on my big day, then she thought no one else should be, either.

With few people showing up to my party besides young friends, I had only a couple of cards to crack open. Those cards were filled with words of congratulations. This clearly meant that I would not have the funds to replace the money my gram had fronted for the food and drinks. That was going to take at least five or six of my part-time fast-food paychecks for me to make good on my word. Thank God my grandmother would be patient. I mentally dug another tally into the deep row of scars my mother seemed to enjoy depositing. *What the hell was I thinking?*

With my boyfriend in the military, it was a no-brainer that it was time for me to follow my dream to go to college and become a teacher. I knew I wanted to start off with a two-year degree, and I searched out a college that offered an early childhood program. My efforts led me to being accepted at a rural SUNY Technology school about five and a half hours from where I lived. It was legit in the boonies. The irony was that most of the students attending there were from NYC, Long Island, or surrounding areas. Talk about culture shock! It was welcomed, however. I enjoyed the vast differences from my hometown and was both curious and delighted to start making new connections that came easily with life on a college campus. We were packed into tiny dorm rooms like sardines. We had no choice but to get to know each other. We were sharing the same toilets and showers, after all.

I should mention that I convinced my "cousin-sister," Heather, to take the leap with me. She was accepted at the last minute, and we were enrolled to begin that fall. I think my grandmother was actually in pure disbelief that I was, in fact going away to college. I did all the necessary paperwork and financial aid myself as an emancipated minor. When I talked to her about it, I felt as if she thought I was only dreaming out loud about something that was not truly a feasible option for me. After all, there were no other college graduates in my immediate family. I would be the very first.

I worked hard that summer to buy myself some dorm room essentials and grew excited about getting away and starting something new. Something for me. Something away from the familiarity of my small town. Soon the day arrived that my aunt and uncle pulled up with a little U-Haul trailer latched to my uncle's piece-of-shit car. I relied on the only vehicle we knew with an accessible hitch to make it happen. Expressing my embarrassment here was useless. Besides, how else would I get to a college hours away from home? I reminded myself to be grateful that my cousin was coming along and that I had this assistance to get my ass delivered clear across the state.

I added my small handful of items to Heather's pile and kissed my grandmother goodbye on her front porch. I could feel how amazingly proud she was of me, even if it did kill her softly to see me go off. In that very moment, it all became real to me. It was no longer a dream. The wheels were in motion, and I knew this was the first day of the rest of my life. Remember: there were no video chats or cell phones in those days. We both knew our only connection would be an occasional phone call to check-in and brief visits on holiday or summer breaks.

The ride there seemed endless, even with all the excitement. The interstate, though pretty, was long, boring, and winding. I remember having to ask to pull over a few times so I could puke. I imagine my anxiety only heightened my already weak travel stomach. I never could make it too far in a back seat without having to toss my cookies. Our college town was nestled deep in the hills of New York. It was a scenic car ride that I would partake in many, many times to come.

When we arrived, there were vehicles parked everywhere on the lawns of the plush green campus. Parents and students were unloading all their brand-new packaged goodies into their microscopic dorm rooms. I was on the fifth floor of a cement building. Heather was on the sixth. There was no sense in waiting for the only elevator, or we would be waiting forever. We grabbed a handful of items and headed toward the steep stairwell. That's when I spotted her: My new roommate, Annie. She looked exactly like the school picture she had mailed me with her welcome letter. (Yes, that is how we communicated way back then!) She instantly made me smile with her ponytail bopping around on the top of her head. Our quirky energies would be a great match.

We still keep in touch today. In fact, I have lasting friendships with several of the people who graced the fifth and sixth floors of that cement hall back in the early '90s. College is one of my most cherished life experiences. I encourage everyone to live on a school campus for at least some time at college. The memories I made in those days are simply priceless. So many songs, foods, and scents can take me right back to a time and place I will never forget.

College also provided me with some cool opportunities that I never would have had in my small hometown. For instance, the time recruiters showed up on campus, soliciting students for summer work. I had no desire to go back home to my grandmother's place for the summer. I had gotten a taste of life away from home. Sure, I missed her and thought of her often, but I also knew there was nothing exciting happening back in those parts. When an opportunity presented itself, you bet your sweet ass I was on board.

Here I was, deep in the mountainous area of upstate New York. The beauty of this natural land was craved by those who lived in the hustle of city life day-in and day-out. The recruiters on campus that day were looking for service workers for a grand hotel tucked in the heart of magical Lake George, a stunning resort for rich vacationers and property owners. Think Kellerman's from the movie *Dirty Dancing*, only more elite and upscale! Heather's roommate, Hannah from Long Island, and I interviewed for positions in the service areas of the resort, and we were handed jobs serving in the dining areas. At nineteen years old, we welcomed the opportunity and the experience. Hannah's parents moved us out of the dorms after our first year of schooling and delivered us a couple hours down the road to a darling little town nestled along the lake. Even though I had grown up on the shores of a great lake, I don't think I had ever seen such a heavenly little vacation town in all my life. Maybe in pictures.

We rented a tiny little cabin right down the street from the spectacular resort, our new place of employment. This hacienda was rustic, to say the least, the type of cabin you would likely rent at a campground. It had built-in bunk beds, an efficiency kitchen, and a working bathroom. It would serve its purpose. Plus, I did not have my own vehicle, so it was important that I be able to walk back and forth to work each day. We were literally just across the street after a short walk across the bridge.

It was fascinating to mingle with the affluent families and couples who walked through the doors each summer day. I felt privileged to serve them and sparked up conversations with anyone willing to partake. They were from so many different walks of life, and there were so many accents! People came here from all over the country. I'll never forget when we servers were asked to work a special event one night, a private party for the truly elite. This required wearing tuxedos and white gloves. We lined the walls of a ginormous white tent, looking like soldiers at ease. When the bell rang, we served or bussed the tables in unison, like something you would have seen on the big screen.

But the best part of all is that Liza Minelli and her live band played throughout the event. I can remember thinking to myself, *Someday I want to enjoy this life.* I wanted to be invited to glamorous parties where people dressed up and sipped champagne served by workers wearing white gloves. It was an experience I will never forget and am grateful to have had. Did I mention we made pretty damn good money that summer, too? All these years later, I still tell myself I'd love to go back there and stay as a guest someday. It's on my bucket list.

It was one of my best decisions to date, going away to college and experiencing a whole different part of New York State. It was my first real understanding of the world outside the walls of my hometown. It gave me a thirst for travel and discovery and the desire to meet people outside of my own zip code.

The Gift

"You can't go back and change the
beginning. But you can start where you are
and change the ending." —C. S. Lewis

While my grandmother was inadvertently teaching me how to be my own hero, she also taught me another super important skill in tackling this thing we call life: independence.

This is another one of those traits that can find itself in the categories of both a blessing and a curse. I couldn't live the life she had, serving dinner and drinks to a husband who'd had one too many whiskey shots each day. Being stuck at home to look at the same walls, all day, every day, and needing to call on a friend, neighbor, or family member to get to places. This was most definitely not a life for me.

I have always, always been one of those I'll-do-it-myself kind of gals. One thing I knew with iron-clad certainty as a young adult was that I would depend on no one, a skill that ripened from birth on, in my case. As harsh as it sounds, I never wanted to find myself in a predicament where I couldn't move forward because I needed someone or something to get me there. Nope, no way. If I wanted something, I worked hard to get it for myself. I took ownership over all that I had or achieved. And while I had some amazing cheerleaders by my side through it all, I still know I am 100 percent responsible for my life and my happiness. My independence.

Self-reliance is a gift that just keeps on giving. It plants the unstoppable seed deep down inside your guts and curates the badass bravery needed to do the hard things. My hyper independence is the reason I made it this far. I depended on myself. When you don't depend on others, you don't feel disappointment. It was another polished layer of armor.

BE who YOU NEEDED when *you were* YOUNGER

—Unknown

CHAPTER 10

Life Calling

NOT TOO LONG AGO, AS my own daughters had grown older and finished out their high school years, I had begun to question them on what they saw for their futures. I was always taken aback when they responded with words like, "I don't know yet..." or when they changed their minds, constantly stating something new or off-the-wall. *What do you mean you don't know?* I just assumed it would be the same for them as it was for me. My contribution to the world was seemingly engraved in my DNA.

I knew at a very young age that I would grow up and become an elementary school teacher. It was in me for as long as I can possibly remember. As a little girl, I would line up my dolls and stuffed animals. In an instant, I would find my "teacher voice" and *voila!* I was shaping the future, one Cabbage Patch doll at a time. I'm pretty sure you could find me in this sort of imaginary play for hours at a time.

Although this is typical play for a little child, I knew it was more than that for me. I visualized myself running an entire classroom of young students. I made maps and room layouts of how I would arrange the furniture and gadgets in just the right order. I made paper lists of the school supplies I'd need to furnish my classroom with style. I subjected any human who was willing to pretend to be my student in preparation for the career of my dreams.

As an adult, and maybe even back then as a kid, I knew my imagination was my saving grace. I could always go inward when I needed reprieve from the vulgarness of the world happening around me. Perhaps it is the very reason I thrive on creativity to this day. Playing "teacher" was both literal and figurative in my little world. I was playing, but I was also teaching myself to navigate life, every step of the way.

My desire to teach was solidified when I entered the third grade. I was placed in a classroom with a male teacher. You might be inclined to think, uh-oh. Not a good fit for a child like me, considering the male brutality I had experienced up to this point in my life. But this male teacher was kind and genuinely caring. A literal savior. His quirky antics and soft voice were like a cozy bedtime story to me.

His classroom was my peace and calm, my sanctuary away from the chaos and craziness I lived in at home. He instantly welcomed us students as if we were truly one big, happy family. He valued each and every one of us for who we were. Our small voices mattered. His room was my first taste of democracy. He never ever made decisions for learning without consulting the students for our thoughts and opinions first.

I remember a crystal-clear example of this. The principal had visited our classroom to deliver a box. Inside the box were samples of potential new science textbooks from various publishing companies. My teacher was told to take a look at them and get back to the principal about which one he'd like to use as the new curriculum for the following school year.

As soon as the principal left the classroom, my teacher asked us all to stop what we were doing and to join him at the round table. We had all overheard the conversation, so we knew exactly what was inside that box. He began taking out the hardcovered textbooks and spreading them around the table. He then said something to this effect: "I am just a teacher. It's not important for me to be drawn to the book. It's important for you to be drawn to the book. I want you students to take a good chunk of time passing these books around to one another. Read the words and check out all of the illustrations. Figure out which one feels comfortable to you as a third grader. In a little while, we will come together for discussion and vote on which one we think will serve us best." And that is exactly what we did.

The more he talked, the more I fell in love with him. Not in a romantic crush kind of way, but more of a paternal or a parenting kind of way. His methods of approaching students were mind-blowing to me. I had never felt that my opinions or ideas mattered whatsoever until I entered his classroom. This man began to show me that I really could contribute to the world, even as a young third grader. He taught me to own my growth and understanding. And I knew I would someday make that same impact. I would provide a safe haven at school for a child like myself, a classroom where children could gather while forgetting the men at home who beat their mothers.

One of the very first tasks I had when entering my college teaching program was to write an essay. The essay instructions were to recall the best and worst teachers I had ever had. It didn't take any thought at all; they were both visible in my mind in an instant. The directions were to write down which characteristics made them the best or the worst. I scribbled a T chart on my paper and got to work creating two lists before beginning the essay. There was no doubt that my third grade teacher was going to get the accolades he deserved here. These words and memories would be recalled easily and joyfully. The other side of the list would obviously be more excruciating. No one wanted to revisit the anxiety perpetuated by the world's worst teacher.

Isn't it ironic that years later, I would be hired as a teacher in the very school I grew up in? My dear favorite teacher would still be there in third grade, putting forth every bit of passion he had shown twenty years prior. It was a no-brainer that when he retired a short time later, they asked me to prepare his retirement speech. I graciously accepted with an enthusiastic *yes!*

In case I haven't mentioned this yet, I grew up in small-town USA, and a good many of the teachers I had for middle school and high school were still holding their same teaching positions. The recognition dinner was to be held at a waterfront hotel. He and a couple of other retirees would be honored in front of more than two hundred teaching colleagues.

I can say with conviction that delivering the speech that evening is one of the most gratifying moments of my entire adult life. You see, in that crowd was not only the best teacher I ever had, but also the worst. My speech opened by telling the story of my task at college on that first day. And you bet your sweet ass I said the words out loud: "Ironically, they are both here in the crowd today." The room gasped. I stated that I wouldn't be spending my time talking about what makes a horrible teacher since everyone in the room already knows. Instead, I set the intentions to tell them about which attributes the best teachers strive to possess. I swear there may have been a standing ovation. I nailed it. And it felt so good for me to look at him and speak the truth of his magnificent impact on my life. I wanted him to know the remarkable difference he made. I cannot tell you the number of pats I got on the back after I finished. My own teaching career would be every bit worthwhile if even one child ever saw me as the saving grace in their life.

And trust me, she knew who she was—the horrible one. Did I mention she hated me because I came from a crumby, broken home full of drama and violence? As if it were my choice. She shamed me and compared me to my older brother on an almost daily basis. He was lucky to be a genius. School came very easy for him, and he was blessed with "book smarts," as I call it. She would address me with, "Your brother never blah blah blah ..."

or "Your brother could do this without a problem!" She would pick and peck at me daily, knowing full well what I was going through in my home life. She was an adult bully. Mental note to self: Never, ever compare a student to their siblings.

In retrospect, I am thankful. They both taught me so much about who I did or did not want to be when I grew up and became a schoolteacher. The impact of a teacher is extremely powerful. I prided myself over the years to be the best teacher possible, reaching and teaching each individual student, just like my amazing third grade teacher.

To this day, my best teacher qualities are fairness and equity. It doesn't matter if you are another teacher's child or a homeless kid in transition. You will get the same amount of care, consideration, and respect from me as a teacher. No favorites allowed.

The Gift

"Be who you needed when you
were younger." —Unknown

I was approximately eight years old when my life calling confirmed itself to me. I would grow to become an elementary school teacher. I never once veered from that decision. I knew this meant years of college. I knew it meant dedication and self-discipline. I knew it meant student loan debt galore. I knew it was to be my life service.

I loved this inner knowing and nurtured it with every opportunity that presented itself. I spent quality time with my little nephews. I worked parttime at a state-of-the-art daycare center located on the college campus. I rounded up the little cousins to lead the games and entertainment any time there was a family gathering. It all came so natural and effortless for me.

Why do I consider this early knowing to be a gift? Perhaps because I know several grown adults who still don't know what they want (or wanted) to be in life. I appreciated having a guiding force behind my decision-making. And although the "what" or "who" I teach might change as the years go by, I will always be a teacher first and foremost. I have faith that the decades of lessons I learned in those public school classrooms over the past years have been quintessential in my personal growth and story. I have received just as many growth spurts as the students sitting in front of me in their desks throughout the years. Our learning never ends. That you can count on.

forgive YOURSELF for not KNOWING WHAT you DIDN'T KNOW BEFORE YOU learned it

— Maya Angelo

CHAPTER 11

Come What May

AT THE TIME I WAS officially hired and began my teaching career, I was a mother to a one-year-old little girl. She wasn't exactly "planned for." I was dating my now husband (off and on), and let's just say she was a sweet little surprise to us both! In fact, when I took the at-home pregnancy test, we were actually no longer living together. We had broken up a couple months prior when he decided he should get his own place. That didn't mean the occasional late-night hook-ups stopped. They very much continued, thanks to my perseverance and unwillingness to accept anything but a lifetime together for the two of us. Remember, I knew it was meant to be when it all started. We would make this work. Somehow. Someway. Although cliché, I have always been a fond believer in the idea that everything happens for a reason. Our time off from one another had never stemmed from any dramatic blowout. We were just typical young lovers who teetered on wanting a stable relationship and also enjoying private time with friends without any constraints. It was a challenge to balance these desires at such a young age.

My pregnancy was nothing short of beautiful, just as I always imagined it would be. I enjoyed every moment of it, feeling ready at twenty-three, to become a mother. Unfortunately, I did spend my last trimester of pregnancy on a college campus finishing out my credits for my teaching degree. I remember I could barely squeeze into those cramped, uncomfortable college desks. I was definitely the only pregnant woman in the class. Probably on the whole campus. But I did not care; I was beaming with blissful thoughts of motherhood and my family to be.

The test stick lit up with a dark pink plus sign. I knew from that moment on it would be a girl. She was the daughter I had longed for since I was a little girl myself. My boyfriend yearned to discover that the baby would be a boy, a son. I think it is fair to say most men dream of a son the way I was dreaming of a daughter, so no judgement here. He got over his disappointment as expected. (Little did he know he was destined to be the father of girls.) One thing was for sure—this pregnancy solidified our love and commitment to each other. It was destiny. She grew on the inside, and our love and appreciation for one another grew on the outside. We had created a brand-new human being together, just as the stars had planned for us.

We did things a little backward. First came the baby. Then the degree and the start of my elementary teaching career. And shortly thereafter, we tied the knot and made our little family official. I was beyond excited to chuck my maiden name aside and assume a new identity as his wife. Trust me, living in a small town meant my story followed me everywhere I went. Having this new, lengthy last name was a welcomed addition to who I was becoming.

We bought a tiny starter home in the same zip code where we were born and raised. In fact, it was directly across the street from my uncle's house. We both worked right in town, and it was decided then that we would raise our children here as well. I had all that I had wished for, just as I planned. Life was happening. It seemed someone had pressed the fast-forward button, as the days began to pass quickly.

Four years later, after frustration and fertility drugs, I gave birth to another baby girl, the spitting image of her sister at the time she was born. We had tried so hard for another baby and felt extra blessed when she arrived. I felt with certainty that her arrival made our family complete. We were a family of four, and I was feeling grateful beyond measure that I was living the life I had imagined for so long. I had hoped to hold onto that feeling of contentment and happiness forever, but we all know life does not play that way. I had spent most of my previous years conquering one obstacle at a time, and now would be no different. New challenges began to come at me faster than the speed of light.

My grandmother, my rock and cheerleader, fell quite ill and her health began fading just after our second daughter was born. It was hard for me to accept and witness her slow, painful death. I suppose it is equivalent to what it feels like to lose a mother, since that is what she was to me. She suffered terribly for several months toward the end, and this put an unwelcome strain on our relationship. I had been her healthcare proxy, a job I wish I never been asked to fulfill. She had opted for a "do not resuscitate" order. But when she began to make a sudden slip, the doctor approached me right in front of her. I reminded him of the choice she had made not to be placed on life-saving machinery, but she viewed it as me giving up on her; putting the nail in her coffin so to speak. She could barely look at me after that conversation. She was never able to speak or get out of the hospital bed again. She withered away with a tube in her throat and bed sores galore for the next couple of months, the very thing she had wished would never happen to her.

Initially, she could communicate by writing on a paper tablet. I remember picking it up one day to see a conversation she was having back and forth with a friend who had come to visit her earlier that day. She told the friend that I had given up on her. It broke my heart into pieces to see these words etched in her handwriting. I did not want to see her suffer in such a way. While her mind was still in order, her body had very much already surrendered. She was battling leukemia and another type of cancer in her sinuses. It was one of the hardest things I ever had to witness, as it physically distorted the features of her face. This incredibly giving, loving woman did not deserve to die such an awful, prolonged death.

I had a needy new baby, a curious four-year-old, a full-time elementary teaching job, nighttime grad-school commitments, and a beloved grandmother dying slowly in a bed out of town. Though I had always managed life somehow, the stress was overwhelmingly winning this time. I was stretched to the max, and it was visible for the world to see that I was losing control. I had my doctor put me on medication for anxiety, as sleep was something I was no longer experiencing with any sort of consistency. The days blended together, and I was in robot mode, trying to make everyone happy in all the places. The medicine did help dial down all the emotions, but I was numb to so many things. Life started to become a blur. I wasn't my best self for anyone, including myself. As a natural-born doer and micromanager, I could not stand to be like this. I felt like I was on the outside looking down at myself, simply going through the daily motions.

I went on like this for a couple of years. I did a great job keeping up the tough task of being a mommy and a full-time teacher. I put on a smile every day and made the best choices I could. Eventually, I knew I needed to stop relying on medication and once again take control of my mind and emotions. I weaned myself back into the world of raw feelings. As I did, I realized that I had also ballooned to well over two hundred pounds in my short, five-foot-two-inch body. In fact, I now weighed more than I did on the days I went to the hospital to give birth to my girls. It is fair to say that food was my go-to for nonpharmaceutical numbing. It always has been. I was a textbook "emotional eater." I spent my entire life as the chubby friend. But it certainly did not help that I came from a family of genetically fat-bottomed girls, either.

It was just around this time that weight loss surgery became popular. I began researching the pros and cons and found that my insurance covered the expense if I met certain qualifications. Lo and behold, I was a candidate. I enrolled in a seminar-style course, a prerequisite to seeing a doctor for consultation. In December of 2007, I underwent elective lap-band surgery. For those who aren't familiar with this, at the time, it was the least invasive procedure where weight-loss surgery was concerned. During this procedure, a plastic device is inserted to encircle and constrict the stomach. It also has a port that sits just beneath the top of the skin. Fluid would be added or removed every couple of weeks via a needle in the port to adjust the tightness and effectiveness of the apparatus.

In just a little over a year, I had dropped one hundred pounds with the help of that amazing device and invention. It was thrilling to experience the energy and vitality that came with shedding such a large amount of luggage from my body. I was like a brand-new person. In all my life, I had never felt so healthy and happy in my own skin. Hands down, it was one of the best decisions I have ever made for myself. I put in time at the gym, followed the given rules, and was committed to making my body stronger than it had ever been. I was fully onboard and did the work necessary to maintain my weight. That is certainly not to say it came easily. Sometimes the lap band didn't work properly. There were times the adjustments were way too tight and other times not enough. Every visit meant needles plunged into my abdomen to try to get it right. Unfortunately, two years later, it would have to be removed in an emergency surgery.

I was outside early one summer morning washing the car in the driveway. I bent over to scrub one of the tires and felt a *pop* inside of me. I immediately saw stars and dropped to my knees on the ground. The circular band inside me had cracked open and was poking sharply at my insides. Thankfully, a neighbor ran to my rescue and drove me to the hospital. I was consequently transported by ambulance to my weight loss doctor and hospital, an hour away. The pain was horrific, and all I could think about was relief. He met me at the hospital and immediately prepped for surgery. I knew what removing the apparatus meant: It meant that I would likely go back to old habits and gain every ounce of the weight back. After all that hard work, I was so disappointed to be in this predicament. Yet, relief was all I could think of in that moment of sheer pain.

Much to my surprise, I had turned my lifestyle and habits around enough to stay on track. Even though the lap band was gone, I tried my best to remember what I had learned along the way. I wanted so badly to keep that healthy feeling alive. I tried hard to stick to tiny portions. I kept up my exercise routine. And the weight stayed off for quite some time. But after a couple of years or so, old habits slowly began to resurface, and food once again became my vice. I turned to it for comfort in everything: sad times, happy times, stressful times. The weight gain took a while but eventually crept right back. I had gained approximately seventy-five pounds. I was obviously disappointed in myself for losing control once again. I was sad that the benefits of feeling so good weren't enough to keep me from self-sabotage. While looking better and thinner was a notable perk of weight loss surgery, I enjoyed the exhilarating feeling of vitality more than anything. The sunshine I had been walking on was slowing fading into the familiar feeling of quicksand.

I knew I had to make better decisions when it came to my health and self-care. I had tasted the victory of optimal health, but it turned out that there would be much bigger fish to fry at that moment in life.

The Gift

> "Forgive yourself for not knowing
> what you didn't know before you
> learned it." —Maya Angelo

It's not all sunshine and rainbows, is it? Some of my gifts presented themselves in rather complex boxes. They would need careful opening. They would sometimes reveal a shiny mirror necessary for self-reflection and a blatant reminder. Self-sabotage reared its ugly head every now and then throughout all seasons of my life, for as long as I can remember. I am guessing this is when the universe decided it was time for me to start taking deep notice of some of these self-defeating patterns that I rather enjoyed.

I am typically a strong starter in all things I do or choose to take on. However, I am an equal "fizzle out-er." I often talk myself out of something before seeing it all the way through, sometimes desperately searching for excuses as to why I should stop or quit an idea—almost as if when things are too good to be true, I would purposefully prevent them from coming to fruition.

I wouldn't learn until much later in life that this stemmed from my upbringing. It is referred to as a fear of success or a fear of being accomplished or at the top. I was intentionally playing small, a stigma I am still working through to this day.

Who was I to be smart? Who was I to do great things? Who was I to have it all? These are underlying questions that would sometimes push my hopes and dreams to the wayside if I neared too close to my desired level of accomplishment. I could probably write a whole book on the numerous things I have self-sabotaged throughout the years. Fortunately, I am also wise enough to know that these very instances are what have made me aware of my actions today. I can almost predict where I will step in and say, "So, you really think you're going to stick with this, Margo?" Self-awareness is the gift that keeps on giving. My inner voice has since resurfaced, and it feels good to be in touch and in constant conversation with her once again. I am thoroughly enjoying the dialog and chatter between my ego and my truest sense of self. There is much to be discovered here if you take the time to tune in and listen attentively.

TURN your *wounds* into **WISDOM**

—Oprah Winfrey

CHAPTER 12

One More Thing

WHAT IS ONE OF THE worst things someone could say to you? A couple things come to my mind when I ponder this question. And unfortunately, one of them came true for me.

You have cancer. Not just any cancer. An extremely rare and tricky cancer decided to grow in my body. The day of my diagnosis is one I will never be allowed to forget. It was a sweltering, hot summer day in August. I was working diligently in my classroom, setting up and organizing for the start of the upcoming school year. New supplies. New themes. New kiddos. I love the smell of fresh beginnings and always have. This is an exciting time in a teacher's life. What I didn't know on that productive Monday was that my life was about to change forever.

The stitches in my head were itching like crazy while I worked. For the most part, I ignored them. But every now and again, I had to sneak in a scratch. It was then that I discovered the bump, or "tumor" that was supposed to be removed, still lingered. This growth that cradled into my scalp revealed to me that it was still, in fact, on the top of my head. I felt perplexed about the stitches and the incision site. How was it that the culprit still presented itself as being in the same exact spot? I was bewildered, but I also knew it would have to wait until my workday finished. I was knee-deep in jungle-theme decor and was determined to get the bulk of it up on the walls and the boards that day before addressing my personal needs.

Just before their 4:00 p.m. office closing, I pulled into the doctor's parking lot. I did not have an appointment to see him. It was my intention to catch him off guard and ask exactly what the hell went on in the operating room just a few days earlier. The nurse placed me in one of his rooms after I told her my concerns. He soon entered, official papers in hand. I will never forget the look on his face. I could tell there was something more to the situation. Something big. I raised my voice, pointed to my scalp, and insisted on knowing why on earth a painful bump was still located on the top of my head!

Stoically, he approached me, referring to the papers in his hand. He babbled something about the reports just arriving "hot off the fax machine." And then I heard it, the *C* word. The one I was not expecting whatsoever. It felt equivalent to a punch in the face. I looked down and saw the verdict there, plain as day, in black-and-white print. At that moment, I felt as if the words were being displayed through a magnifying glass: adenoid cystic carcinoma.

Everything went black. Literally. I'm sure it was only for a moment, but it felt like an hour. My ears were boiling with heat. My face was flushed. Tears dripped onto my lap in an instant. *Did this really just happen?* Turns out, he had removed the tumor completely, but there still might be residual cancer in the surrounding area, as it appeared to have been infected. He immediately escorted me in my confused state out of the room and to the front receptionist. I was sobbing hysterically. Uncontrollably. People were watching me, peeking around their magazines to see what the fuss was all about.

The doctor told his aide to get me the information for the closest cancer institute. I went numb and could not move or breathe without effort. The receptionist felt my pain while trying to keep her composure and write down the information for me. I sensed her pity as she tried to do her job. She then paused and told me to just go and that she would have the hospital contact me directly, so I didn't have to stand there in shock any longer. Time stood still. It was that same feeling you get the moment your children are born—only on this day, it was not welcomed. Not at all. *Why was this happening to me?*

I walked to my car in the parking lot. I don't know how I managed. My legs were weightless. I couldn't feel anything. I can only remember hearing the sound of my sobs ringing in my head. I shuffled to find the keys and opened the door so I could just sit. I took several deep belly breaths, as I truly believed I would hyperventilate. I hated the feeling of being so alone in that moment. There was nobody to hold me up, rub my back or blot my tears, or to tell me I would get through this. I searched frantically for my cell phone and dialed my best friend, Sarah. She is an experienced registered nurse who could naturally give me the words I needed. I could barely get the word *cancer* out of my mouth. She could not understand me through my bawling. And when she did, she was far too in shock to react the way I needed her to. I hung up and called my husband next. He reacted with the same disbelief in his voice. "What do you mean? Are you sure? Who told you this? Where are you?" he asked.

I did a hard wipe across my face and eyes into my sleeves and turned the key to start the car. Thankfully, I was exactly one mile down the street from my home. In retrospect, I was driving while impaired—impaired by a possible death sentence and one that would not let the tears stop, even for a second. I couldn't see straight, but I didn't care. I only wanted to be home with the people I loved. At that time, on that Monday afternoon, it was just my two daughters, aged eleven and fifteen. My husband was out of town working for several days.

I am certain they were scared to death as they saw me crumble apart right before their eyes. I kept saying it out loud, over and over again: "I have cancer. I have cancer!" While most parents might take the time to deal with this privately and compose themselves, I am not most parents. I exude emotions and have spent my entire life displaying them for the world to see. Today would be no different. I felt impending doom, and those poor daughters of mine did as well. But I selfishly needed them at that moment. They were my comfort. My reason for pulling myself together.

How could this be happening? How could it possibly be cancer? Yes, I'd just had a tumor removed. But the same doctor had removed three previous tumors from that exact location over the past several years. Each time, pathology had come back as a benign cylindroma, which my doctor told me we didn't need to worry about and that it was nothing more than a crazy fluke. I had never worried once. The symptoms and timing of this tumor were precisely like the last ones, so what made it cancer this time around? Slide comparisons would soon reveal it had been cancer all along, a misdiagnosis by our local hospital's pathology department. I'd unknowingly had cancer growing and recurring in my body for the past eight years. Eight fucking years.

The hours that followed involved tedious internet searching. I say tedious because, if you type in the words *adenoid cystic carcinoma* into a search bar, you are not going to like what you find. Words like *rare*, *aggressive*, and *unknown* will be the first you'll stumble across. It is considered a glandular cancer, so why did it choose to grow on my skull, underneath the layers of my skin? Of the billions of hits the word *cancer* could bring up, I could find only minimal information on my diagnosis. Even worse, I could locate only one other case of this cancer being found on the scalp region. My feeling of impending doom skyrocketed to heightened levels.

Everyone warned me to stay off the internet. We all know it can be our best friend or our worst enemy. And most of us don't bear the credentials to diagnose or predict treatment. But somehow, searching Google gives us the power to do just that. Since my intake appointment at the cancer institute was scheduled for a whole three weeks out, I had plenty of time to pollute my mind with worry and a possible death sentence. Rightfully so, since technically this cancer had lived, misdiagnosed, in my body for almost a decade now. Did I mention my original surgeon refused to remove the stitches for fear there was more cancer lingering? That meant nearly a month of these plastic stitches embedding themselves into my sore, itchy, cancer-ridden head.

I was grateful and relieved when the scans and tests revealed the cancer was only in this one odd area. The doctors were perplexed, as adenoid cystic carcinoma usually originates in places like the eye, soft palette, throat, and so on. They were preparing for the spot on my scalp to be a metastasis from a primary location. So at least for the time being there was that one silver lining. It did not appear to have spread from somewhere else according to the PET scans.

A team of doctors agreed that the only logical step of action would be to remove a large area of the scalp, down the bone, on the top of my head—a nearly four-inch circle that would be scraped down and then filled with a skin graft taken from my thigh. The staff at this renowned hospital had never once seen ACC in this site before. I would later learn that I was only one of seventy-four cases reported worldwide to date. *Really? I'd rather boast those odds while winning the lottery, for Pete's sake!*

While I waited another several weeks for a surgery date to open up, I traveled to another state's renowned cancer institute for a second opinion. Although I felt trust with the first doctor, it was just being smart to hear the words come for another educated surgeon on the matter. My bestie, Sarah, and I packed an overnight bag and headed one state over to a renowned clinic in Ohio. Turns out, the doctor there, who was seasoned in some rare ACC cases, was also perplexed. He agreed fully with the game plan and the operation my local surgeon had proposed to attack the cancer site. It was decided then that I would seek treatment closer to home and stick with the original doctor. The next few weeks were long and agonizing, but the surgery day finally arrived.

I had a humongous team of cheerleaders in the lobby. Great friends, my husband, my daughters, my mother-in-law who had flown in, and even my mother and younger brother were present. It was a scary time, to say the least, and fear had the best of me on that morning. *Would they find that the cancer had penetrated to my skull bone, which would indicate they may need to drill through to my brain area?* This was an actual possibility, and I had to sign a waiver stating that I had agreed to this extensive change of plans should they stumble upon these findings once they went in.

Amen. I had been granted the best-case scenario. I woke to the news that the tumor removal had, in fact, taken all traces of the cancer. The large area was still scraped and removed as a precaution since the tumor had regrown four different times in the past years. I stayed overnight, and my bestie, the nurse, curled up beside my bed to be with me. The plastic surgeon who performed all my reconstruction was a Godsend. He created a medicine bag of sorts filled with ointments and potions for sealing and healing the skin graft crater that now sunk into the very tiptop of my head. It was sewn with stitches to the top of my scalp to keep it from any sort of movement. I vividly remember looking into the mirror the next day and seeing what appeared to be a bird's nest or a large blooming onion sitting on my head. It was awful! Not to mention my bright blonde hair was now colored red with all the dried blood. It hurt far worse than it even looked, but that strange medicine ball contraption thankfully worked its magic, and the skin graft "took" as we had hoped. I was so grateful for his torturous concoction after all.

I wasn't mentally or physically prepared for how horrifically painful a skin graft would be. My upper thigh, where the skin was borrowed, felt like fire. I was so focused on what it would be like to lose the top of my head. (I had even cut and shaved my own hair off the night before surgery just so it wouldn't be such a tremendous shock.) In my opinion, the skin graft was equivalent to a third-degree burn—a stinging, ringing pain that would not let up whatsoever. When they removed the bandages ten days later, I thought I might take someone's head off. Removing the gauze layers was like ripping away a layer of me. One of the staples holding it in place was twisted and was not cooperating as it should. They had to do some serious work to get it out of my skin. I was growing stronger by the minute, I tell you! That was a procedure I wouldn't wish on my worst enemy. They say that what doesn't kill us can only make us stronger. Ain't it the truth? I should be fucking invincible by this point.

The healing took a long, long time. There would be several more reconstructive surgeries over the next couple of years. My plastic surgeon would slowly remove pieces of the skin graft to regenerate my scalp. The sad news was that my sick time at work had run out, and I needed to return. All the progress was halted and put on hold for almost another two years before we began reconstruction surgeries again.

I found myself lucky in that chemo and radiation were not part of my prognosis. They were not effective therapies for treating my type of cancer. However, the tradeoff was a series of rigorous reconstructive surgeries, and reconstruction was no easy feat. I had implants, just like saline breast implants, placed on top of my skull. For six months, they lay between my skin and skull bone where they were filled with increasing amounts of liquid to precisely stretch my skin and hair follicles in order to prep for massive reconstruction. The tenderness of my growing head created uncomfortable sleep for months! My poor head was unmistakably shaped with hills and valleys. All I could think of was the pitiful movie I had seen as a child, *The Elephant Man.* My head wasn't too far off. Thankfully, I had an amazing and accommodating surgeon who did a wonderful job bringing my head back to normal after those brutal skin-stretching procedures. I trusted all his decisions, and he always respected mine. I am happy to report that all the hair on my head is my own! (Even if we did have to chop my scalp up like puzzle pieces and reorganize it to create a brand-new head of hair.)

I am over seven years out now from my official cancer diagnosis. Some would say that puts me in remission, but this type of cancer does not follow those rules. It has a mind of its own and often rears its head when least expected. Still, I wholeheartedly consider myself a thriver after cancer. It is in my past now. Another notch in my journey to becoming the me that I am. Just another successful obstacle tackled and noted in my book of life.

I would never say I welcomed its lessons. But it certainly taught me a thing or two about myself and the world around me. Most importantly, it afforded me the reminder that there is a silver lining in just about anything life throws your way. If you sit down and take the time to connect the dots of your timeline, your inner knowing will guide you to see how it all leads to the bigger picture.

The Gift

"Turn your wounds into wisdom."
—Oprah Winfrey

When I was first diagnosed with cancer, there was a particular quote that people would share with me. It even landed itself on the team shirts my supporters would be wearing in my honor. It read, "Tough times don't last. Tough people do." Sounds like a perfect slogan for a badass obstacle-slayer such as myself. I know they chose it with the best of intentions, believing it encapsulated my very essence. But secretly, the quote did not speak to me. It made me feel sad and even ashamed of my recovery. I had met many cancer warriors in several social media groups, badasses such as myself. Some of which did not make it. *Weren't they tough enough? Would I be any different? Or would my toughness not matter at all in the end?*

I quickly had to coach myself out of that attitude and defeated way of thinking about my situation. When I turned within, I was reminded that we are all worthy of redemption. I was reminded of the million challenges I had already overcome in my lifetime. I was led back to my faith, my core beliefs, and values for the first time in my adult life. I prayed moment to moment, not because I feared, but because I had an inner knowing that everything was going to be all right. I could see it. I could feel it. I knew it to be so. These thoughts of reassurance were nurtured over and over. I prayed because I was grateful. This would be another one of those mountains I would have to climb with blood, sweat, and tears to prove to myself that, with faith, I could handle any challenge or moment of adversity needing to be faced.

My spiritual roots and inner knowing had begun to resurface. This was the actual beginning of my awakening. Cancer was in my cards as part of the journey, a reminder of who I am and who I am not—not as a punishment for something I had done, as I originally tried to convince myself. But rather as a catalyst to reintroduce myself to that which I already knew.

I am loved. I am guided. I am worthy. Always.

doubting *yourself* IS NORMAL. LETTING **it** STOP YOU *is* a CHOICE

—*Mel Robbins*

PART III

The Awakening

CHAPTER 13

Game Changers

WHEN I BEGAN THINKING ABOUT writing this book, there were going to be only two parts. I had not a clue that Part III even existed. In fact, I now know that Part III is the reason the book was written in the first place. As I mentioned in the preface, I knew the release of my story could be as much of a healing journey for me as it could be for you. I wanted to share the tools that ushered me to the other side of those mountains, only I really didn't know how that connection was going to come about until the chapters began to flow. It all unfolded right before my very eyes, an understanding of why I was meant to share my story in the first place.

After my cancer journey turned into survivorship, things in my life took on a new perspective. It was as if Phase Two had officially begun. I obviously appreciated life and all the little things it entailed more than ever before. Oddly enough, that is the blessing that comes with life's hard lessons, such as beating cancer. I believe in my core that this is something not usually experienced until you are shaken so deeply by something as blatant as impending death. During those initial days, every possible scenario played out in my head. I could not bear the thought of my daughters growing older without me. I could not bear the thought of not getting a chance to become a grandmother to their children. I could not fathom the thought of my husband going forward alone. And that is exactly what created the strength I needed to push forward and put it all behind me. For that, I am truly thankful.

One thing you learn when you are laid up because of a setback or illness is that life always goes on, with or without you. It was a tough pill to swallow at first, watching the world proceed smoothly without me as I spent time in constant recovery mode, healing in bed or on the couch. But it no doubt opened my eyes to witness the perspective and lessons my soul had been searching for.

Little did I know, life had a few more curve balls it wanted me to swing at in order to further grow and awaken my light. Aside from cancer, most of my adult "growing pains" came from self-inflicted choices. Right after my bout with cancer, I decided I needed a change in my career. I bravely bid into a fifth grade teaching position after being a primary teacher for seventeen years. I felt it was time for something different. Time to reinvent myself as a teacher.

I couldn't have possibly been more excited. I spent countless hours preparing my classroom that summer and spent hundreds and hundreds of dollars out of my own wallet to decorate and to buy materials and resources that would help me to be the best fifth grade teacher ever. My mindset and intentions were absolutely in the right place. Only one problem: as it turns out, I am *not* smarter than a fifth grader.

The year started off with a bang! I immediately loved my students and felt it would be a breath of fresh air working with kiddos who could do things independently for a change. What I didn't realize was that fifth grade common core math was going to be the life of me. This was no joke. I had completely forgotten (or was in denial) about my fear of numbers. I had sucked at math my whole life. It was another one of those school subjects where I would never outshine my older brother. Numbers were perceived as impending doom as far as I was concerned.

I often had panic attacks when it came to crunching numbers for real-life scenarios, especially when I was put on the spot. When my daughters' coaches would ask me to run the Little League candy stand, I would practically feel like fainting. *Um, no, but my husband will do it!* The thought of tiny kids waving their hands at me with handfuls of loose change needing to be calculated in lightspeed was enough to send me over the edge.

Within the first few days of my new fifth grade position, I hung my head and went to my administrator in actual tears. I begged for a transfer. There was no way in hell I could make this work. I have always prided myself on being an amazing teacher. Here I was, totally incompetent to teach these children what they needed to learn. I felt like a complete failure and fraud for the very first time ever in my life. *What had I done?* The transfer was denied, and I had no choice but to stick with my decision. I was locked into at least 180 days of this curriculum with the hope that a vacancy would present itself the following year.

Most people, including my immediate circle, were oblivious to just how derailed my life became in a short amount of time. It's all because I am great at putting on my smile and trudging through. Hell, it's literally what I have known my whole life. This obstacle would have to be more of the same. I put my game face on and prepared to suck it up. I must say, with certainty, my year in the fifth grade took more of a toll on me than fighting cancer, both mentally and physically. At least with cancer, I had an inner knowing that everything was going to be all right. With my grade level change, I feared I may end up in the Betty Ford Clinic.

I spent every single night in the beginning months crying out loud to my husband. That poor man sat next to me as I watched countless instructional videos online, trying to learn the best way to deliver these hour-long math lessons each day. None of it made sense. Not even a little. I was doomed. I was trying to unravel all the mathematical learning I had acquired over my lifetime to make sense of common core thinking. After a couple weeks of doing this, depression and defeat came settling in. It quickly got to the point that I went to my primary doctor and had her prescribe medication to deal with my unraveling. I knew my only hope was to numb it out. The thought of pretending to be a fifth grade math teacher each day crippled me. For the first time ever in my teaching career, I felt sick to my stomach just pulling into my parking spot each day. I hated my career. I hated my life. It made me physically ill.

Enter my new best friend, wine. I had always enjoyed wine, spirits, and socialization on the weekends. But I was never, ever, an at-home "solo" wine-drinking kind of girl. It got to the point that I would absolutely need at least two glasses of wine before pressing play on the instructional videos I tortured myself with every evening. The sheer thought of sitting down to them each day brought me into the fetal position. I couldn't even eat. I shrunk down to the lowest weight I had ever hit, as alcohol became my saving grace and the way to survive the entire school year. I consumed it daily to void my feelings and to get by. I consumed it to sleep without anxiety. Or so I thought.

I feel the need to insert a small disclaimer at this point. To look at me, you never would have known I was dealing with the notion of incompetence and a volatile inner critic. I put a smile on as I entered those school doors daily. I am a professional, and never in a million years would I let those students know that I was dying inside a little each day. I did, however, confess my academic weakness and let them know that I was learning every bit as much as they were.

When the math block arrived each day, I looked up answers in front of them. I created teams to troubleshoot and solve things we were unsure of. And in the end, it ended up being a huge growth year for all of us within those classroom walls. Our room was full of uncertainty and risk-taking, a skill we can all benefit from building upon. I taught them as they taught me. I praised them and thanked them along the way. We had a remarkable year, even if the curriculum itself was not bringing me personal daily joy.

The challenges I faced from that one year in fifth grade took my healthy "social" drinking to unacceptable, scary levels. Even after surviving and seemingly thriving through that dreadful year, the drinking didn't stop. I had adopted a new way of living, a new way of celebrating and coping. A new daily habit and tolerance to alcohol that wasn't going to go away. One or two glasses of wine easily turned into a whole bottle. The need for a bottle then turned into the need for a bottle and a half. This was a slippery slope, considering the long line of alcoholics I came from. I didn't like this new dependency one bit, and I wasn't in denial of it. An unhealthy addiction was created, and it continued for quite some time. That dependency finally changed when an eye-opening opportunity literally fell into my lap.

Up to that point, I had never in my life been someone who read a book for pleasure on a regular basis. In fact, I have always admired my friends who read constantly for escape. (We can thank that dreadful elementary teacher for stealing my love of reading.) I am way too busy for the type of relaxing it takes to devour a good read. But that all changed for me when a couple of friends recommended some appealing titles. I made time for some page turning and was grateful that I did. One book in particular was about to change my trajectory and my entire way of life. My current way of living, thinking, and being would pivot in a brand-new direction as a result of inhaling a memoir. It came recommended by my best friend, who said the main character reminded her of me.

With piqued curiosity, I purchased the book *A Happier Hour*, by Rebecca Weller, on my Amazon Kindle. And just as my bestie alluded, I soon found myself completely relating to the main character. I quickly became consumed with the words on the page.

This chick had a similar issue and style of indulging in alcohol, drinking to oblivion and then having blackouts. Drinking as a means of self-sabotage. The more she described her life, the more I realized mine was pretty much going in the same direction. Life was becoming a series of hangovers and *Oh, shit, what did I do last night?* Not a pretty picture for a schoolteacher or a mother of two growing young ladies. It felt as if I were looking into a mirror and seeing a crystal-clear reflection of myself for the very first time.

I have lost people I love in my family to alcoholism. I have shut people out of my life because of their existing alcoholism. And yet, here I was, potentially heading right down the same path. This book was the answer. It was the catalyst and mirror for the changes I needed to adopt, and it had all happened in almost an instant. With the turn of the last page of her book came the next chapter of my life. Literally.

The author made a pitch at the end for an online support program she created. For about $200 US dollars, you could join her ninety-day sobriety challenge. It was a coaching course of sorts with daily encouraging emails to keep you on track. It entailed correspondence from the author herself, interviews with other sober gals, recipes for mocktails, and links to countless other resources to check out for sobriety support. I clicked and added that opportunity to my cart without even a second thought! Two hundred dollars? Hell, I was spending way more than that on my favorite wine and liqueurs each month. This was a personal investment I was ready to make. Usually when I take on something like this, I set a "future" date to get my head in the game and mentally cheerlead and pump myself up. However, that was not the case this time, and that is how I knew I was serious. I was starting the very next day. It would be my day one of the ninety-day commitment. I had no idea at the time that this would be the greatest personal investment I would ever make for myself.

Anyone who has ever tried to get and stay sober knows just how much of an effort it takes. There is a huge level of self-loyalty required to play a hand in your daily efforts. This journey back to inner strength and commitment looks different for everyone. For my father, a severe alcoholic for decades, it was "cold turkey." He literally just woke up one day and said *no more*. He has now been sober for nearly thirty years. For my older brother, it was the support of Alcoholics Anonymous meetings that led to his sobriety. He is soon approaching eighteen years sober.

For me, it was reading a recommended book that helped me to see myself in the mirror for the first time. It was a deep-seeded desire to be a better role model for my two daughters. It was refusing to live the way my mother had. It was finding more productive ways to spend my free time. It was searching out healthier options for sleep and relaxation that weren't harming my body and mind. It was opening daily inspiring emails and watching interviews of women in similar predicaments vowing to change their lives. And it was learning new coping skills that would teach me to address the stressors and triggers the booze had masked on any given day. That little ninety-day program did not disappoint. I was led to just the right people and resources I needed for the metamorphosis taking place. I was a sponge. The more I read and learned and clicked new links, the more I wanted to heal myself and lean the fuck in.

I have accomplished many things in life. I know what it is like to feel proud and successful. I hold a master's degree in education after rising through the ashes of childhood hell. But I had no idea that embarking on sobriety was going to be so much more than just a three-month challenge.

It was a gateway to a better way of life, the next part of my life. It opened doors to a whole new world. My sobriety challenge continues, even as I write this book and celebrate over two years sober. The things that have transpired since that day in August are nothing short of miraculous and welcomed. All the questions, all my life trials, all the hurdles and obstacles, would soon begin to make sense. I'd only begun to scratch the surface.

Sobriety helped me sleep. Sobriety helped me gain clarity. It forced me to slow down and take a deep look within. It challenged me to seek what I might be suppressing. It caused me to peel back the underlying issue of my overeating and overdrinking. The more I uncovered truths about myself, the more I wanted to heal and feel better. These limiting beliefs and bad habits of mine were formed over years of chaos and instability. I now knew I had the power to change all of this. I listened to podcasts. I read more books. I subscribed to empowering blogs. I "liked" people and places on social media that promoted my new uplifted way of being. I began meditating and writing (even just a little) every single day. I spent time with my inner self and my deep thoughts. I welcomed the energetic vibrations and calming powers of crystals and essential oils into my home. I began trusting and experimenting with my intuition. I gave myself permission to let go of negativity and toxic people. I set hard boundaries to preserve my energy. I began to feel significantly more peaceful than I ever had experienced before.

Most importantly, I let go. I no longer felt the need to control every little thing in my life. I now understood why my need to constantly control everything had come about in the first place. I had never experienced or witnessed it in my childhood. For most of my life, things were entirely chaotic. Therefore, I had let it become my obsession as an adult to control whatever situation I could. With sobriety, however, I was now free to begin living for the day, enjoying the present moment instead of festering on the past or worrying about the future. Believe me when I say that it's the most wonderful feeling in the world. There is pure peace in slowing down and taking notice.

Turns out, sobriety was another catalyst for change waiting patiently within me—the true awakening necessary for this book to be born and brought to life. I had let go of the reins for the first time ever. I knew with certainty and clarity that I was not the one in control. I released, allowed, and trusted in the beautiful transformation happening within and around me. It was as if the universe had suddenly said, "Let's get this girl sober. She has some questions, and she is ready for the answers."

Everything was happening in perfect order. Divine timing. The sobriety challenge allowed for this book to come to life. To be unleashed from deep inside of me. The writing of this book allowed for my spirituality, beliefs, and inner knowing to fully resurface once again. I was to be reminded of who I truly am. Every meditation, mantra card, podcast, article, book, and online course brought me one step closer to rediscovering the me that I am.

The Gift

> "Doubting yourself is normal. Letting it
> stop you is a choice." —Mel Robbins

You have likely noticed that repeated patterns of self-sabotage have not yet fully exited my life. And while I cannot wait for the day when I will say that I am no longer a self-saboteur, I also cannot deny the learning that comes with being able to take notice of it. There is always, always some gold to be discovered when we sift through the aftermath.

Fortunately for me, perseverance was a skill I had already mastered. And there would be growth and nuggets of wisdom that would stem from this obstacle, just as with all the others.

The following fall, I was able to bid back to a teaching position in my previous building. I would be teaching second grade for the first time. And although it wasn't the grade level I preferred, I knew I would be much more comfortable facilitating learning for younger students. While working to prepare my classroom for the start of the school year in September, the telephone rang. When I answered, I found my previous administrator was on the other end of the line. I couldn't imagine what he would be in touch about. I had hoped to leave the fifth grade debacle behind me.

He called to tell me that the state had finally released the scores of the previous year's standardized testing, and that my classroom of students had earned the highest-ever math scores the school's fifth graders had ever achieved. The grin on my face felt frozen.

When I hung up the phone, tears streamed down my face for two reasons. One, he could never know how much that phone call meant to me or how much I needed to hear those words. I so desperately needed to know that my time and struggle truly made an impact on those students, regardless of how uncomfortable it made me feel for all those months. But most importantly, it opened my eyes. It had been one of the most vulnerable seasons of my entire life. By modeling my vulnerabilities for those students to see, they were able to rise to the occasion of their own education and growth. I would often bravely confess to them that I did not know the answer and that we would need to figure it out together. For the first time ever, I wasn't standing at the front of the room spoon-feeding knowledge into the young brains before me. Rather, I transformed into a facilitator and problem-solver right alongside them. An equal. And together, we did it. My vulnerability led our way through as they forged the path ahead.

While I was trying to stay afloat that entire year, one of my most embedded limiting beliefs was being challenged and healed. I had spent an entire lifetime telling myself that I was not smart enough. I told myself stories about how I would never understand mathematical concepts. I would convince myself to never consider being an entrepreneur because of my fear of numbers and calculations.

The universe had provided the opportunity to show me otherwise. I can and will do hard things with grace and grit.

I am... TWO of the most POWERFUL words FOR WHAT you put after THEM shapes your reality

—Bevan Lee

CHAPTER 14

Finding My *Why*

ONE OF THE VERY FIRST things you are asked when you proclaim you are writing a memoir is, *Why? Why write a book and tell your story? What are you doing it for?* And these are certainly valid and important questions. Why would someone want to dish out their personal narrative for the whole world to see? I actually wanted to write this book for several reasons.

First and foremost, it started out as a means of healing. I imagined physically removing the story from "inside" of me and downloading it to an "outside" storage unit of sorts. I would create a vessel where the stories could be referenced, while trying to make sense of all that had shaped me. Putting the contents of my life within the pages of a book creates a concrete monument for anyone observing my trials and triumphs. This would be a location to visit and witness the me that I have become. (At least up until this point, as my journey is a lifelong endeavor.)

Second, I have always been comfortable using my voice to speak and share. I even received an A+ in my college public speaking course. Conversation and persuasion come naturally for me, mostly because I am enthusiastic about the things I share and speak about. Passions can be contagious and create connections.

Connection then leads to self-discovery. I have always longed to have talks and discussions about my resilience and perseverance. I want others to know and understand that our circumstances are always temporary. We do not have to be given the power from someone else to depict our outcomes in life. I would love nothing more than to help others understand and accept their fullest human potential, and to rise above and do better than what they currently know.

Finally, I needed to write the book to find the answer to a burning question that has long plagued me and even made me feel guilty at times throughout my life: *Why me? How did I get so lucky? Why did I get to grow up successful, happy, thriving, and motivated, when my two brothers both faced much more difficult paths to adulthood?* We were raised in the same exact circumstances, after all. We had the same shitastic start in life. We bore witness to the same horrifying events for years and years as young children.

Things never came easy for any of us. The comparison game had always burdened my reasoning when my siblings came to mind. It just didn't seem fair that I was the one flourishing. I also held bitterness about the fact that I was not only lacking parents in the truest form, but I was also robbed of growing, thriving relationships with my siblings because of the less-than-ideal circumstances we had grown up in. I didn't get to bond with my brothers the way I should have. Initially, we were protectors of one another. But as the years passed, we became hardened and self-involved. We later learned to protect ourselves by tuning family life out. In essence, the child abuse, neglect, and domestic violence had robbed us of creating loving relationships with each other in our younger years.

I will not share any of their stories here. It is not my place to represent their perspectives or recollections of our childhood years. But I will say, it was this burning question of wonderment that led me to the spiritual awakening I am experiencing even as I write this book. This download of "inner knowing" had finally resurfaced, so I can fully understand why my brothers and I were not experiencing life the same or why we didn't respond to challenges in the same way, didn't learn and grow from our circumstances in the same way, and why our lives are on completely different, estranged paths as a result.

Who knew it would take a sobriety challenge to bring about the answers and catharsis I had been seeking for so many years? In fact, I didn't even know what I was looking for until now. Lo and behold, the universe brought me to other answers and even more clarity that would be necessary for true inner-healing work that needed to be done.

There were so many things I needed to figure out. You know those perfect families, the ones that seem to have it all together? The ones that seem to spew unconditional love and acceptance? The ones where Mom and Dad are living in pure bliss while each kiddo grows up to be flawless and successful? Turns out, they don't exist.

Yes, we get our DNA from our parents, whether they are the ones who raise us or not. And those who do parent us certainly shape most of our beliefs and patterns in our earliest years. But ultimately, as I have proven, none of that matters, really. I believe, whole-heartedly, we all have a predetermined purpose here on earth, one that even our family dynamics cannot alter. In seeking answers, I was simply reminded of something I already innately, deeply knew.

We are here having a human experience. We are all souls with a predetermined map of purpose to seek out and fulfill. We are all spiritual beings with blueprints all our own.

For me, the search was over. It all came full circle and was ready to be discovered, or rediscovered, if you will. It is all still a bit of a shock to me. This awakening led me down the path to my inner knowing, a place that already existed within me, yet wasn't unleashed until now. It was not new information. It was a recalling of that which I already knew.

As I mentioned previously, the sobriety challenge came with coaching emails. The author provided a few paragraphs of personal motivation each day, and at the bottom of each one, she typically included more resources to click for further exploration. While her words and personal accounts were always deeply inspiring to me, it was the "resources" she gave that opened a whole new world of possibilities.

I would discover authors, coaches, bloggers, and speakers I had never heard of before. I subscribed to new sites. I enrolled in virtual summits that hosted renowned speakers who riffed on topics about self-compassion and spirituality. I began to deliberately tap into my inner wisdom.

I was born and baptized Roman Catholic, though I never considered myself a "practicing" Catholic. My mom made sure we all participated in religious classes until the third grade, not that she was a holy roller by any means. It was just something you did in our little city. Once we finished our Holy Communion, it was as if church was never mentioned again, and we were doing the bare minimum to be allowed into the pearly gates once the time should come. I may have attended Mass here or there with my grandparents or perhaps for a holiday, but I was never properly educated in religion and could only tell you the rules, as opposed to any history or understanding, sadly, to this day. I have no hard feelings against religious groups. I just found that I personally did not identify with any specific one.

I have always believed in God as the highest power. I have also always believed in life after death, and that we are souls having a human experience that doesn't end once our bodies give way. It is no surprise that there has always been an element of spirituality inside of me. I grew up and still live just miles down the road from the world's largest spiritual community, Lily Dale. It is a small village of sorts, inhabited by renowned mediums from all over the world. The grounds are magical and visiting the residents will likely make a believer out of any skeptic.

I remember listening in when my mother spoke of going there for "readings" when I was very young. As soon as I became old enough, I booked my own appointments or visited with friends to have a session that could connect me with the "other side." I never once had a bad experience. I often received vivid messages from my spiritual guides. They say the more open you are to these beliefs, the more spiritual guidance will become available to you.

Even with curiosity and spontaneous visits to the spiritual community down the road, I was never dedicated to any regular practice or prayer, per se. In fact, prior to sobriety, I would classify myself as one of those people who only dropped to their knees to pray when situations became dire. I didn't have any faith in universal source energy and had no prior knowledge on the topic whatsoever before I quit drinking. In my most recent years, I wanted to belong to one of the local church communities. However, it just didn't feel right to adopt rules in order to fit into any religious group.

My sobriety challenge resources began leading me to names like Gabby Bernstein and Louise Hay. I absorbed their books and resources, finding them to be fascinating and inspiring and oddly familiar. Before I knew it, tapping into these authors soon led me to many other inspiring names. There was a common theme being delivered and downloaded to me: self-love and the law of attraction. I will admit that I had heard the term before—I had even heard of the movie and the book, *The Secret*, many moons ago. But it was nothing I ever investigated or acted upon. Now, I suddenly could not get enough of educating myself on the matter. It was as if a weight had been lifted from me. I was making sense of the beliefs I held down at my core. I was understanding and uncovering more and more about who I was. I was gaining knowledge about how to use new tools, such as meditation and my own intuition, to navigate life and have faith in all that is happening around me.

My only question was, why now? At forty-six years old? I certainly could have benefited from spiritual grounding all those years when my life was on autopilot, and I didn't have much faith in life's outcomes. And then I got my answer: A true spiritual awakening can only occur when you are one hundred percent ready to receive and believe. As a complete control freak, micromanaging everything, numbing out pain and stressors with booze, I was blocking my own access to the knowledge deep within. It took sobriety and a much calmer Margo to release control and to allow, to see, to feel, to connect with a higher source, and to realize nothing happens "to" us; it all happens "for" us. My deepest needs and truest desires had begun to surface. I simply wasn't ready to notice the signs in the past when my kids were younger and life was so hectic and blurry.

And suddenly, I began learning about my soul and the "soul journey" of others, answering the questions I had held inside of me for so long. My mother, not being able to mother, was never about me. It wasn't the fault of my siblings. It wasn't particularly about the home she was raised in, either. It was about her soul blueprint and what she was meant to live and learn in this lifetime. *Her* purpose. Sure, her lessons certainly affected me. I won't discount the trauma they created in my life for way too many years. But this new knowledge and enlightenment is what I needed to finally forgive her and to understand that it has always been part of the bigger picture. She was destined to be a mother who couldn't love in this lifetime. I was destined to be a child who would not know a mother's love. There was no changing what had already been decided. The only control we have is the way we react and proceed forward with what we are dealt in life.

And this led me to a much deeper understanding of the "me that I am." Loud. Happy. Boisterous. Optimistic. Giving. Creative. Loving. Controlling. Evolving. These are all purposeful attributes of my life experiences, and I wouldn't change them for the world. My brothers have their own soul blueprints as well, purposes all their own. Their journeys are not the same as mine. Their lessons are nowhere near the same. And while we were meant to be siblings in this lifetime, we were each born to check off different experiences while embarking on this list called life.

This new knowledge I had gained (or refreshed) from absorbing amazing content from the likes of Gabby Bernstein, Ainslie MacLeod, Wayne Dyer, Bernadette Logue, Marianne Williamson, Louise Hay, Mike Dooley, Emma Mumford, and Eckhart Tolle would soon set my mind and spirit free, quite literally. It lifted the guilt I had long carried around about the estranged relationships I had with my parents and siblings. It gave me the insight I needed to leave the toxicity behind. It affirmed that I had lived through the necessary lessons. And most importantly, it was time for forward movement.

But that is not the only epiphany that came to light. Revealing what I had already known down at my very core also solved several other riddles in my life. I learned so much about myself. My actions. My evolution. My triumphs and mistakes. And in turn, I began to love and forgive myself with each passing day of my growth. My awakened "inner knowing" also helped me understand so much about myself as a mother as well. I had always wondered why my own two daughters were entirely different. (Not that it's a bad thing.) They simply had notably different relationships with us as parents. We thought we had given them equal love and support throughout life. We had spent years wondering why one kid liked this and the other did not, why one showed emotion and the other did not, and why one was highly motivated and the other not so much.

I had to be reminded that I am their mama. They have my DNA, love, and support. But they also have souls. They have souls on their own missions with life lessons to conquer in their own unique ways. I have helped raise two unique individuals who will approach and savor life in two completely different ways. My awakening has brought total peace to this understanding and to our household dynamic. I will always love and encourage them from the sidelines, but I have since learned to let go of the reins. Letting go has brought a sense of peaceful release in so many areas of my life.

Sobriety = Awakening = Inner Peace

If you would have told me a two years ago that I would no longer be drinking, I would have laughed in your face. My life had centered around social drinking for the past thirty-plus years. If you would have told me a year ago that I would be connecting with my inner, higher self and trusting in the universe, I would have told you that you were crazy. Prayer and pause were something I had never taken the time to explore. If you would have told me that my book would finally be written and birthed, I'd think you were joking. *Who am I to write a book?*

Yet here I am, sober, calm, focused, and writing the freaking chapters of my story.

The Gift

"I am ... Two of the most powerful
words; for what you put after them
shapes your reality." —Bevan Lee

What does gratitude mean to you? What are you grateful for in your life? Personally, I never understood how deeply grateful I was for my life up until this point. Sure, I was thankful to be alive. I was thankful I didn't stay on the path my parents had paved. I was thankful I knew better and did better (most of the time). But it wasn't until I truly rediscovered myself that I began to understand my own depths of gratitude for this life. To be married and loved unconditionally. To serve and teach children in my own hometown. To be the mother of two fabulously different daughters. To have a home I adore being in each day. To empathetically acknowledge that there are many in this world who aren't as fortunate as I am.

My journey taught me that gratitude isn't just about finding the good stuff. True gratitude must also acknowledge the ugly, messy stuff, too. I certainly did not go about life as some saint, void of err. I made plenty of mistakes as a child and even as an adult. However, there are no regrets. Some of my worst decisions brought about my biggest growth, and I am grateful for the uncomfortable lessons that taught me who I do or do not want to be, even though it was difficult to imagine at the time.

Gratitude is the ability to see the good that is already around us and focus on it. The ability to acknowledge the good that can rise, even from despair. Though gratitude was always there for me, I now cultivate daily practices that have helped me to grow this important skill on a much deeper level. There are many research studies out there, including a popular one from the University of Berkeley that prove repetitive practices, such as keeping a gratitude journal or even just having discussions at the dinner table each day about things to be thankful for, can help reduce stress and anxiety and promote better sleep.

For well over a year now, there hasn't been a single day that has gone by that I didn't take the time to write about the gratitude found in the reflections of the day. Take note: There is always, always something to be grateful for. I am grateful. I am worthy of having things to be grateful for.

153

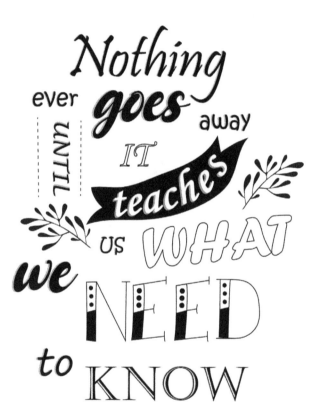

Nothing ever goes away UNTIL IT teaches us WHAT we NEED to KNOW

—Pema Chadran

CHAPTER 15

Yellow Brick Road

I HAD MENTIONED THAT RIGHT around the time I had officially begun this book's outline, I also decided to start going to therapy. I know, I know, you are probably thinking that should have happened long ago. And I couldn't agree more! With all this trauma and dysfunction, formal counseling really could have helped throughout my life. But for whatever reason, it wasn't in the cards until this point. I began researching certified counselors in my surrounding area. I didn't want to just sit and spew my story on someone's couch; I wanted someone who would have more of a holistic approach. More specifically, I wanted a practitioner who was certified in EFT, also known as Emotional Freedom Technique, called tapping. Tapping was a technique I had learned about during the beginning stages of my sobriety challenge. This is a self-help tool to use on oneself in times of uncertainty or anxiety. It involves self-talk and specific touchpoints on the body. After a bit of researching, I found a practitioner who was not only certified in EFT but also used techniques such as Reiki and sound healing. I couldn't wait to get started, even if I had to drive an entire hour to get to the appointment.

I immediately felt comfortable and at ease in her presence. After four or five sessions, I knew we were beginning to scratch the surface, going back to the days of little Margo. I have no doubt we were on our way to some potential breakthroughs. These sessions brought about tears and strong memories, but then something rather unexpected happened. Surely it was a blatant sign from above. The universe was sending me strong signals.

I was driving alone in the car one day, listening to a podcast recommended by a good friend. The speaker was Kara Lowenthiel, who bills herself as a life coach and mentor with a potty mouth. She has a give-it-to-you-straight type of approach. In fact, her podcast is appropriately named *Unfuck Your Brain*. To me, she was exceedingly easy to listen to. Her dry sense of humor and crass advice were just the things I needed to hear that day. During this particular episode, she began to explain what it is she actually does and what her type of coaching was all about. More importantly, she began talking about how coaching was different from traditional therapy. My ears perked up and my inner knowing dialed in. I knew with certainty the message she was delivering at that moment was undoubtedly meant for me to hear and ponder.

In a nutshell, she explained that therapy focuses on the past, whereas coaching focuses on the future and forward thinking. It was as if a lightning bolt had struck me. My jaw actually dropped down in amazement at this *aha!* moment. I didn't want to spend time reliving my past. I would much rather focus on what was yet to come. I could feel the endless potential and possibilities right in front of me.

Let me also state here that she did not discount the benefits of therapy and that there are many people who, in fact, need to work on issues of the past. (Yes, I am clearly one of them.) But it was in that moment when I realized I did not want to be one of them. At least not then, though possibly in the future. I didn't want to go back to all those days of horror and sadness. I knew, with conviction, that I was meant to move forward. Coaching was the right next step for me. Not only did this moment clarify what next "right action" I needed to take for myself; it cleared the path to discovering my own purpose: to coach and teach others. I could immediately feel myself in her shoes while she spoke. I realized that I already was a life coach. Heck, I had a top-notch, real-life degree in it as far as I was concerned. I had been coaching myself for over forty years. Now I just had to make sense of it all and organize it. It is my purpose to give others guidance and inspiration, using my own years of experience as proof that we become the choices we make day-in and day-out.

As cliché as it sounds, this whole journey reminds me of *The Wizard of Oz*. Seriously! Dorothy ultimately journeys back to self-awareness and what she had known all along. I could feel myself clicking my own pair of ruby red slippers. I had come full circle, too. Through it all, I always held the tools and knowledge to overcome, rise above, and refuse to play victim, to know I'm loved by a higher power, and to know I have an important role and place in this world. I had come to realize that each of us has this knowledge deep within us if only we are willing to allow it.

Turns out, I had been manifesting my life's outcome all along, only I didn't even know what *manifesting* meant until I started my sobriety journey and began reading everything I could about the subject. Modern day guru, Gabby Bernstein, states that "manifesting is cultivating the experience of what it that you want to feel and then living and believing in that experience so that you can allow it to come into form." The law of attraction was at work for me. Suddenly, so much was clear. I had created this. I literally paved the way for all I wanted to achieve in my life. I purposefully shaped my life and willed its unfolding. I was "future tripping" as a young child. These forms of coping and self-soothing, these visualizations, and the playfulness within my own imagination were what ultimately saved me from being stuck in that repetitive, generational cycle of a miserable life. I am responsible, one hundred percent for where I am in this moment of my life.

A flashback of proof downloaded gracefully into my mind as I wrote this chapter. I was to be reminded that I had the power all along, as if a portal had sucked me back into a moment in time. Just like Dorothy awaking from her daydream, I was looking down upon myself in my grandmother's house.

There I was, sitting on her living room couch, a giant catalog tucked between my knees. I was flipping through the pages of the Sears Christmas Wishbook. (Oh, how I loved when that catalog would arrive in the mailbox each year!) I would sit down and get right to work. In this vivid memory, I must have been about six or seven years old. I was circling items with a pen and also creating a paper list to keep track. My grandma came close to see what I was up to. She asked about my list and whether I was getting it ready to send out to Santa. Then she leaned in closer and realized what was going on.

I explained to her that the list was not for me; it was for my daughters. I told her how I didn't want Santa to deliver these items to me. I wanted him to save them for my daughters when I had the chance to be a mommy myself someday. She felt the pain and longing from all those years of neglect in my home. She grabbed me and held me tight, the kind of hug that feels it will never end. I am pretty sure I spotted a tear or two in her eyes as she looked down upon me. My innocent eyes stared deeply back into hers.

At the time, I had no idea how endearing or powerful that moment was. (I am so glad I get to relive its beauty now through memory.) I was subjected to some ugly times back then, but in the safety of my grandma's presence and home, I dreamed of the day I would have my own loving family and about how I would do it all so differently. I would do it right. I was manifesting my deepest desires. I was visualizing the outcomes of my future self at such a young age! And I never, ever lost sight of my hopes and dreams. I held tight to the energy connected to those visions and aspirations. I knew how much my husband and I would love each other. I could see our home and yard, our children, daughters, lovingly playing together within it. I saw my classroom setup, where I would spend my days as a teacher, loving God's other children and making them feel cared for and loved. It was a crystal-clear mind movie that I played over and over until it was literally brought to life over the course of several decades.

The more I read about it, the more I understood the law of attraction and how it had been exactly what I was doing all along. And the best part was, I realized it didn't have to stop there! Another amazing *aha!* moment had just come to surface. I had accomplished each and everything I had set out to do as a young, hopeful little girl. Every single thing I dreamed up and pictured in my mind had come to life. And now, as a middle-aged woman, I was prompted to see that there could be more to come. It was time to dream and visualize beyond the here and now. It was time for more hopes and manifestations to create the next level of me. It was time to continue down my path and even deeper into my purpose.

So much has happened to me in the past year or two. I like to think of the first half of my life as the prep work for my amazing future. Excitement overcomes me as I mentally design what is yet to come. Could it be the tattoo I treated myself to for my birthday that unleashed the call of the universe, when I permanently inked the words of Paul McCartney on my leg, "let it be," a theme that has no doubt been serving me throughout the sobriety and book-writing journey this past year or two? I have been surrendering and letting go, trusting in the universe wholeheartedly. And *ta-da!* Magical things are transpiring for me.

The Gift

> "Nothing ever goes away until it teaches us
> what we need to know." —Pema Chodron

My spiritual awakening has been a blessing in so many ways. It feels as if someone handed me the keys to any doorway I choose to open and explore. Each day, I notice more and more signs and synchronicities that prove life is all about energy and frequencies and finding our vibrational matches.

I was driving down the interstate recently, listening to a broadcast hosted by Sonia Choquette, a great intuitive. At one moment, she was talking about the subtleties of signs and synchronicities and how to be more aware by using your intuitive guidance. Just then, I looked up at the RV driving steadily ten feet in front of my windshield. Its nickname was displayed in bold, bright colors across the entire back of the camper: "Enlighten." The word *enlighten* was quite literally staring me down as she began telling the story of enlightenment. My jaw dropped open, and then I smiled with acceptance of the message that had just been delivered to me on that drive.

A spunky spiritual guru known as Noor Hibbert calls this "tuning-in to the Universe FM." We can all dial into the frequency of this channel if we choose to pay attention. The signs are out there for all of us. It just boils down to our willingness to see and believe and receive. My intuitive tap has once again been turned on, and I will do everything in my power to stay tuned into "Universe FM" and trust that I am always receiving.

By the way, I looked up the definition of *enlighten* later that day when I was sharing the story of how the word came to me at such a particular moment. *Oxford Dictionary* describes it as a verb that means "to give someone spiritual knowledge or insight." Mind blown. It was the gift of all gifts. The culmination. The understanding that universal flow and love has always been here at my disposal. An endless tap and a beautiful reminder on that particular day.

the universe buries STRANGE jewels DEEP within us all, AND THEN STANDS BACK TO SEE if we CAN FIND them

—Elizabeth Gilbert

CHAPTER 16

Pain to Purpose

IT SHOULD COME AS NO surprise that as I typed, wrapping up this book, my mother succumbed to her internal and physical struggles and passed away, almost as if I were given the green light to birth my story and bring it to life.

Her death made me question the stability of my inner peace and knowingness. I was undergoing the truest of tests. My spiritual awakening was being provoked. All I had recently learned and come to understand was challenged as people in my life began to insist that I may want to rethink my choice of not going to her bedside for some sort of closure. What they didn't understand was that my experience was not theirs. They likely did not know they were passing judgement through their own limiting beliefs when they said such things aloud to me. They had no idea about the inner work and transformation that had occurred within me to prepare for this very moment.

I had recently been reminded of deeply buried knowledge about soul journeys and soul contracts for a reason. I knew with certainty the one between my mother and I had already expired. At least for now, in this lifetime. Though I felt deep pity and sadness, I was committed to my inner peace first and foremost. I knew that seeing her was not going to close any wounds or mend any broken hearts. Those wounds had been healed and forgiven by me, over time, through tears and personal growth. I had let go. Our soul contract had expired years before the death of her physical body and being.

Actually, my mother died a long time ago. Perhaps when I was born. Maybe even before that. She died when she was seduced by a life of mental illness and addiction, and she didn't have the strength, tools, or determination to overcome it. And in the end, my mother ended up being my greatest teacher in life, teaching me everything I never wanted to be. I would learn to grow and thrive and love and be the exact opposite of her.

As I drove in the car just days before her death, waiting for the unavoidable news, Audible was playing a chapter from Glennon Doyle's book *Untamed*. I was enjoying every ounce of her story but was particularly enthralled hearing her read the pages of a chapter entitled, "Boulders." Her words created a perfect summary of what I had recently come to understand about the ebb and flow of love and my relationship with my mother.

Glennon wrote:

> *This is what I know. Parents love their children. I have met no exceptions. Love is a river, and there are times when impediments stop the flow of love.*

> *Mental illness, addictions, shame, narcissism, fear passed down by religious and cultural institutions—these are boulders that interrupt love's flow.*

> *Sometimes there is a miracle, and the boulder is removed. Some families get to experience this Removal Miracle. Many don't.*

> *All the love in the world cannot move a boulder because the Removal is not between the impeded and the ones*

who love her. The Removal is strictly between the impeded one and her God.

My mother didn't have one boulder. Her river of love was impeded by a wall of boulders. Sadly, my family would never come to see the miracle removal happen for her in this lifetime. We had all certainly hoped and prayed for years that it would. It is my sincere wish that in my mother's next lifetime, her river of love flows as graciously and generously as the one I have been blessed to bask in all these years, despite never knowing a mother's love.

I have forgiven her and have chosen, rather, to acknowledge that the life lessons she inadvertently taught me are, in fact, *the legacy* she leaves behind. I am a biproduct of her boulder-blocked river. I, myself, am filled with love and light because my mother endured decades of darkness. We can share love and light with others only when we ourselves are filled with the self-love and acceptance of who we are.

So how did I do it? How did I survive all this childhood trauma and grow up refusing to repeat the pattern as so many do? How did I cultivate the mindset and momentum to put myself through school and college? Where did I find the strength to beat and rise above a rare cancer diagnosis? What told me it was time for a medical intervention when it came to my ever-growing body? Why was I able to just wake up one day and proclaim that I would no longer have a relationship with alcohol, even after decades of relying on it for my ups and downs in life? Where did this innate knowing that all is well and will work out just fine in the end come from, anyway?

I spent my entire youth emotionally orphaned. I had a mother and a father who were completely inept when it came to parenting or nurturing me. They were both incapable of choosing their children before themselves. This naturally showed me how to become my own parent. I learned to love and nurture myself. I learned to do things for myself. I learned to provide for myself. I worked tirelessly as a child to fill all the voids I knew needed tending.

In writing this book, so much has been revealed about my path. Not only did I heal; I awakened to my true self, my purpose. I came to understand that the universe has been in charge all along. Each tiny piece of my life experience had been precisely orchestrated as I was guided forward. Each person was carefully chosen to see me through life's ups and downs. Writing this book has revealed to me that I have spent a lifetime collecting or creating precious gems for my internal toolbox—the same box that housed a deep-seeded knowing that there is more to life, and that I would be granted the journey forward to claim it. The secret box that held these coping mechanisms is the very reason I have made it this far in life without a complete breakdown, tools I have been able to tap into for as long as I can possibly remember. These are the silver linings granted in return for our strength and perseverance in times of despair and challenge.

Call it what you'd like: unlocking the door, connecting the dots, putting the puzzle pieces together, being handed the keys to the kingdom. I had just witnessed my own life come full circle right before my very eyes, a true awakening, and I had pages upon pages of writing laid out before me to prove it was so.

The Final Gift

They say that with every storm comes a rainbow at its clearing. My life has undoubtedly been a series of shitstorms that have left behind tiny pots of gold. Treasures that could be cherished for an entire lifetime and perhaps even beyond. Seems like a fair trade. I have finally taken the time and have done the work to remember who I truly am, the me that I am meant to become in this lifetime. As I have said before, I wouldn't trade any of it. I am fully aware and appreciative of the nuggets of wisdom life has handed me through its lessons—good or bad, happy or sad.

I have fully accepted, since early childhood, that life will always be about trial and error, mistakes and lessons, fear and failure, and triumphs and growth. But life is also mostly about what it is we choose to do with those hidden gifts found inside of each of those personal lessons.

I look forward to my next chapter and the one after that. I know, wholeheartedly, I am exactly where I am meant to be. I know I am loved and guided. All is well and precisely as planned. I have found my gifts, and now I dutifully share them with the world. My growth and evolution will continue as I encourage and inspire others. These tools are available to everyone, at any age. They are always there to utilize and to count on. We simply must notice and acknowledge their power. We must show the world how to stay in tune and connected to one of their greatest strengths and resources.

I think Elizabeth Gilbert nailed it with her words of wisdom: "The universe buries strange jewels deep within us all, and then stands back to see if we can find them." I love nothing more than discovering new jewels and then proceeding to figure out what it is I am meant to do with them.

I encourage you to seek out your gifts. Dig for your buried treasures. Never stop digging.

the
MEANING OF LIFE
IS to **FIND**
YOUR | GIFT
the PURPOSE
of life is to
GIVE it *away*

— Pablo Picasso

ACKNOWLEDGMENTS

He wasn't named in my dedication, but the truth is, I could never have written an entire book without the love and encouragement of my husband. From proofreading the pages I had written, to listening to potential chapters read out loud, he was there for me every step of the way, always believing in my capability and worth. Thank you for your selflessness and for being my best friend, my amazing husband, and an outstanding father. We are lucky to have you.

To my accepting in-laws, who have steadily provided the family life I longed for all these years. Thank you for welcoming me and embracing my children with love and devotion.

To every family member, dearest friend, neighbor, or colleague who clicked to open and read one of my blogs or email messages, I thank you. Your interest and support are what motivated me to keep moving forward when I may have been hiding behind an inkling of doubt that I could ever be a *real* author. Your belief in me will never go unnoticed.

I must also thank the multitude of experienced influencers out there who helped me bring my tiny idea to life. I was fortunate to embark on writing my memoir during a global pandemic, a time when many famous names began sharing their content and resources online. Without their free or discounted workshops and master classes, I would have never known when or how to get myself started. Your guidance and direction have been essential to my journey as an author.

And lastly, to whomever it is who reads this story from cover to cover, please know that I am eternally grateful. I am grateful that you somehow identified or were touched by my story. I know we are all challenged with adversity and dysfunction to at least some degree. How we choose to respond and to cope is what ultimately makes us who we are, who we aren't, or who we are yet to become. Keep believing in yourself. You, too, are meant for so much more.

RESOURCES

Book Writing

Shannon Kaiser, www.playwiththeworld.com.
Azul Terronez, www.authorswholead.com.
Gabby Bernstein, https://gabbybernstein.com/bestseller-masterclass-waitlist/.
Emma Mumford, https://emmamumford.co.uk/authors/.
Andrea Owen, www.yourkickasslife.com.
Amy Ahlers, www.wakeupcallcoaching.com.

Spirituality

Bernadette Logue, www.thedailypositive.com.
Gabby Bernstein, www.gabbybernstein.com.
Emma Mumford, www.emmamumford.co.uk.
Noor Hibbert, https://thisisyourdream.com/.
Wayne Dyer, https://www.drwaynedyer.com/.
Louise Hay, https://www.louisehay.com/.
Marianne Williamson, https://www.marianne.com.

Books

Rebecca Weller, *A Happier Hour.*
Jamie Kern Lima, *Believe It!*

Glennon Doyle, *Untamed.*
Noor Hibbert, *Just F@#king Do It!*

Podcast

Kara Lowenthiel, *Unfuck Your Brain.*

9 781982 279363